D1560740

UNLOCKING ESTATES IN LAND AND FUTURE INTERESTS

■ ■ ■

by

Michael V. Hernandez
Professor of Law
Regent University School of Law

AMERICAN CASEBOOK SERIES®

Mat #41625258

American Casebook Series is a trademark registered in the U.S. Patent and Trademark Office.

© 2014 LEG, Inc. d/b/a West Academic
    444 Cedar Street, Suite 700
    St. Paul, MN 55101
    1-877-888-1330

West, West Academic Publishing, and West Academic are trademarks of West Publishing Corporation, used under license.

Printed in the United States of America

ISBN: 978-1-62810-038-9

ACKNOWLEDGMENTS

This book would not have been possible without the assistance of others. During my 2011 Property course, I mentioned in passing that I was thinking about drafting a workbook on Estates in Land and Future Interests, and my students' exhortations to do so, both in person and in their evaluations at the end of class, motivated me to undertake this project. I am grateful for the support my graduate assistant, Joshua Smith, provided in drafting and editing earlier editions for class use and finalizing the print edition; I could not have completed this book, certainly not as quickly or as well, without his exceptional work. Another graduate assistant, James Wheeler, provided invaluable assistance drafting problems, proofreading, and editing earlier editions. Students in the 2012 and 2013 Property classes provided helpful comments on earlier drafts. My colleague, Eric DeGroff, graciously agreed to use a draft of this book in his class and shared numerous insights on how to improve the text. I remain indebted to my mentor and friend, Wade Berryhill, who has served as a role model and from whom I have learned much about teaching Property and law in general.

SUMMARY OF CONTENTS

TABLE OF CONTENTS

UNLOCKING ESTATES IN LAND AND FUTURE INTERESTS

CHAPTER 1

INTRODUCTION

■ ■ ■

Suppose you own a tract of land called "Blackacre." You wish to convey Blackacre to a friend. What property interest do you currently own, and what property interests can you transfer? Can you place conditions on your friend's ownership of Blackacre? Can you control how long he owns Blackacre, or who will receive it after him?

This book answers many of these questions, providing an introduction to and in depth analysis of the law of *present estates and future interests*, the system that governs the interests that can be owned and conveyed in real property. Before beginning this study in earnest, several preliminary points are in order.

First, the material covered in this book is conceptually challenging. It involves terminology and concepts rooted in feudal English history that are foreign to most Property students. There is a logic and flow to the material, but it is not always intuitive. This material is best mastered by doing problems, rather than case analysis, although the concepts learned through problems will lay an essential foundation for analyzing real life disputes in casebooks. This unique area of law is a bit like a combination of math, logic, and foreign language. For some students, that is exciting, and for others it is daunting. But any successful law student who studies this material diligently can master it. Don't listen to the naysayers who suggest otherwise! Also, regardless of your legal interests or aspirations, this study will challenge you to practice close and careful analysis—a habit that will serve you well in any field of law.

Second, this book is the study of conveying real property. If Oscar owns Blackacre, he might convey it to Albert. Using letters for simplicity, we say, *"O to A."* A letter in a conveyance in this book represents a living person. For our purposes, O is always the original owner who has full title to the property. A person who conveys a property interest by deed to another is the *grantor*. Some of the examples and problems in this book will involve a party seeking to transfer property by a will rather than by a deed. In those cases, we presume that "T," the *testator*, is the original owner with full title. Other letters (such as A, B, and C) represent either the name of the party to whom a property interest is conveyed (*the grantee*) or other individuals referenced in the conveyance (for example, O could convey Blackacre to B until C's 18th birthday).

Third, it is important to distinguish the basic categories of interests encompassed in this area of law. A *present estate* is a property interest that entitles the owner to present possession and use. A *future interest* is a property interest that the owner presently owns but where the right of possession and use is delayed until a future time, after the current present estate holder's interest ends. To draw an analogy, imagine a parent with two children who want to play with the same toy. The parent says, "Child 1, you can play with the toy from 12:00 to 1:00, and Child 2, you can play with the toy from 1:00 to 2:00." At 12:00, Child 1 has both the right to play with the toy and the present possession of it; at 12:00, Child 2 has the right to play with the toy at 1:00, but not the current possession of it. Child 1 has what is similar to a present estate, while Child 2 has what is similar to a future interest.

Consider another analogy. If you are leasing a house during your first year of law school, you have the present right to possess the property. But your landlord has not parted with title to the house, and he will be entitled to use and possess it when your lease expires. The landlord's future right of possession follows your present right of possession. Your lease—known as an estate for years[1]—is a present estate, and your landlord's right to future possession is a type of future interest. The lease documents probably do not explicitly state that the landlord has the right to possess his house when the lease expires. But common sense dictates this conclusion: a grantor who does not convey all of the grantor's rights to the property implicitly keeps all rights not conveyed.

Fourth, the law governing estates in land and future interests originated in English common law, which our colonies and states inherited (except for Louisiana, which inherited the French civil law). The material that follows will refer to the original common law rules and to modern rules that have modified the common law.

Finally, there are four attributes of property rights (some property interests have more attributes than others):

- The right to use and enjoy the property and exclude others.

- The right to convey the property, either by sale or gift (***alienability***).

- The right to leave the property by will (***devise*** the property) to a person or entity (***devisee***). This attribute is ***devisability***. (The ***testator*** devises property to the devisee.)

- A person who dies without a will and owning property dies ***intestate***. A state statute designates the person or people who take the property by ***intestate succession***. The person who takes the property at death if the decedent does not have a will is the decedent's ***heir***.[2] The ability of property to pass by intestacy is the attribute of ***inheritability***.[3]

Under the common law, owners were not free to create just any interest but were limited to specified options (this is known as the ***numerus clausus*** principle). In the next chapter, you will learn three present estates in land—the ***fee simple absolute***, ***life estate***, and ***fee tail***—and two future interests—the ***reversion*** and ***remainder***. You will learn other present estates and future interests in subsequent chapters.

At the end of each chapter, there are Practice Problems that reinforce the lessons learned. The answers to the Practice Problems are in Chapter 11 at the end of this book. Following the Practice Problems, there are additional Class Discussion Problems that test your knowledge of what you have learned. To enable your professor to go over these problems in class, the book does not provide answers for them. In order to master this material, you need to study the chapters carefully and work through all the problems in each chapter.

With that introduction, let's enter the wild, wonderful world of estates in land and future interests.

---

[1] An estate for years—a lease—is a *non-freehold* estate. The estates covered in this book are *freehold* estates. You will learn more about non-freehold/leasehold estates elsewhere in your study of Property.

[2] An intestacy statute provides a priority list of heirs. If a person dies intestate and is not survived by anyone listed as an heir in the statute, the state is designated as the final heir; in that instance, the property ***escheats*** to the state.

[3] Contrary to common (mis)usage, an *heir* does not *inherit* under a *will*. Instead, a *devisee* receives property under a will. An *heir* only *inherits* in the absence of a will. Moreover, a person's *heirs* do not exist until that person dies, because an heir must survive the decedent in order to inherit his property.

CHAPTER 2

FEE SIMPLE ABSOLUTE; TWO EXPIRABLE ESTATES AND THEIR RELATED FUTURE INTERESTS

■ ■ ■

We first turn to three basic present estates—the fee simple absolute, the life estate, and the fee tail—and two future interests—the reversion and the remainder.

A. FEE SIMPLE ABSOLUTE

A fee simple absolute ("fee" for short) constitutes the ultimate interest in realty, or "full" title. The common law required the following language to convey a fee simple absolute:

O to A and his heirs

The phrase "and his heirs" signified that O was conveying full title, a fee simple absolute, to A. For conveyances to an entity, such as a corporation, ***and its successor and assigns*** was the language necessary to convey a fee. In the conveyance above, A is the ***purchaser***, and "to A" are the ***words of purchase***. On its face, this grant may seem to convey the property to A and his heirs collectively, but that is not what the words mean. "And his heirs" is a phrase of art, known as ***words of limitation***, signifying a fee simple. Think of it this way—it is not presently possible for O to convey property to A and his heirs collectively because A does not yet have any heirs—heirs are survivors who take property when A dies without a will, and they cannot be ascertained until A dies. Instead, these words of limitation signify that A's full title will continue after A dies, passing to his heirs if he still owns the property at his death and dies without a will. More specifically, this phrase was the common law's way of saying "to A in fee simple." The common law strictly required the phrase "and his heirs" to create a fee simple.

Today, the phrase "and his heirs" is not required to convey a fee simple absolute, and the law presumes a grantor intends to convey his full title unless he makes it clear he does not intend to do so. Under modern law, if the first grantor, O, owns a fee (which we will presume throughout this book), it is assumed O intends to convey his full title unless he makes it clear he wants to convey less. Today, the following conveyances are presumed to convey a fee, absent clear intent to the contrary:

O to A in fee simple

O to A

Because the fee is the ultimate interest in realty, unless an explicit limitation is placed on the use of the property, the only restriction is that the owner of the fee cannot do anything illegal with the property (e.g., create a nuisance). The holder of the fee has the full present interest by law for as long as he chooses to own it, and he also has the right to determine who gets the interest after he dies. Thus, a fee is:

- *Alienable*: The holder of the fee has full title and can freely dispose of it, i.e., sell or give title away. This illustrates why "and his heirs" are merely words of limitation that describe the grantee's interest; they do not grant an interest to the heirs—the heirs have no right to stop A from selling Blackacre. For example, your father may own valuable realty, and he may have left it to you in his will or you may presently be the likely heir by statute, but that does not mean you are guaranteed to get the property when he dies; he has the right to sell it or give it away.

- *Devisable*: A's interest in Blackacre does not die with A—this reflects that a fee is full title with no inherent ending. If the owner still owns the fee at death, he can leave it to whomever he chooses in his will—his devisee.

- *Inheritable*: If the fee owner dies without having conveyed the property to anyone and without a will designating who gets the property at his death, the property goes to his heir by intestate succession. A's heir—whoever that will be, determined by statute when A dies—will take Blackacre when A dies owning Blackacre without having left it to someone else by will. The common law system for determining one's heirs was known as "primogeniture" and was based on the Canon of Descent. Today, heirs are determined by state statute. For simplicity, we will simply refer to "A's heir" as the person designated by controlling law to take A's property by intestate succession, when A dies without a will.

B. EXPIRABLE ESTATES

The fee simple absolute is full title indefinitely; the owner can enjoy the property for his lifetime and determine who gets full title at the owner's death. By contrast, two other present estates, the life estate and the fee tail, are inherently **expirable**, which means they can end and thus will not necessarily exist indefinitely.

1. LIFE ESTATE

A life estate is an estate for someone's life only and thus is expirable because it will end when the person dies. At common law, because the phrase "and his heirs" was required to create a fee, a life estate was created by default as a matter of law when the grantor either did not make the intent to convey a fee simple absolute clear (e.g., "*O to A*") or when the grantor failed to use the correct terminology to create a fee simple (e.g., "*O to A in fee simple*"). Today, because the grant "*O to A*" is presumed to create a fee, and the phrase "and his heirs" is no longer required,[1] a life estate is usually only created expressly, e.g.:

O to A for life

It is also possible to create a life estate measured by the life of someone other than the grantee:

O to A for the life of B

This is known as a *life estate pur autre vie*. B is the measuring life and owns no property interest. A owns a present estate in the property for as long as B lives.

A life estate has the following characteristics:

- *Alienability*: Because a life estate only gives the grantee the right to possess and use the land for a life, it expires at the end of that life. It is therefore alienable only to the extent of that person's life, the interest the grantee has. If A owns a life estate, and he conveys it to B, what does B have? B owns a life estate pur autre vie for the life of A. The life estate will expire when A dies; A cannot convey more than he owns.

- *Inheritability/Devisability*: With one exception, a life estate is neither inheritable nor devisable. Because a life estate expires at the owner's death, when the owner dies, he has nothing to leave by will or for an heir to inherit by intestacy. The sole exception is that a life estate pur autre vie is potentially inheritable or devisable if the person whose life measures the estate is alive when the owner of the interest dies. Assume A owns a life estate for the life of B. If B dies before A,

---

[1]   This book follows the modern approach and thus does not require the words of limitation ("and his heirs") to create a fee simple. However, "O to A and his heirs" is still effective to create a fee simple. Because this terminology is still common, some of the examples and problems in this book will use "and his heirs" to signify a fee simple.

A's life estate expires at B's death. If A dies before B, the life estate has not yet expired, but the owner, A, is now dead; who owns the interest? The common law established that this life estate nonetheless expired at A's death *unless* A's grantor, O, made it clear in his grant to A that the life estate was inheritable (e.g., "*O to A and his heirs for the life of B*"). This language made it clear both that the estate exists only as long as B is alive, and that the life estate is devisable or inheritable if A dies before B. The common law referred to the devisee or heir who takes the life estate at A's death as a *special occupant*. If there were no special occupant, then the first person to take possession, the *general occupant* (essentially a squatter), would take the rest of the life estate pur autre vie. Today, a life estate pur autre vie is presumed to be devisable and inheritable even if it was not so expressly stated. Thus, in the original example, if A dies before B, A can leave the rest of the life estate in his will to his devisee, and if A does not have a will, then A's heir will own the life estate for the rest of B's life.

2. FEE TAIL

A *fee tail* is a form of a fee, but only the grantee's bodily heirs ("*issue*") can take the title after the grantee dies (adopted children are not heirs of one's body). The fee tail thus provided a way for the grantor to make sure the property would stay in the grantee's bloodline. At common law, the language used to create a fee tail was

O to A and the heirs of his body

or

O to A and his bodily heirs

Like a fee, the words of limitation ("and the heirs of his body" or "and his bodily heirs") do not vest A's bodily heirs with a property interest; those words simply signify a fee tail. A alone is the purchaser and owner of the fee tail.

Today, as with the fee simple, specific words of limitation are not required to create a fee tail provided the grantor makes his intent clear. Under this approach, the following language would create a fee tail:

O to A in fee tail

There are variants of the fee tail—the fee tail special:

O to A and the heirs of his body by W

This fee tail will only continue beyond A's death if A has at least one bodily child by W.

The fee tail male:

O to A and the male heirs of his body

And the fee tail female:

O to A and the female heirs of his body

And, of course, there can be combinations of the above, such as a fee tail special/male:

O to A and the male heirs of his body by W

Unlike a fee, and like a life estate, a fee tail is potentially *expirable*—it will run out if/when the owner dies with no bodily heirs (no remaining issue).

The fee tail has the following characteristics:

- *Devisability*: A fee tail is **not devisable**. Because the property must go to A's bodily heir at A's death, A cannot leave it to someone else in his will.[2]

- *Inheritability*: A fee tail is **inheritable only by bodily heirs**, i.e., direct lineal descendants (issue), and these heirs also take only a fee tail, ensuring that the fee tail will remain in A's bloodline as long as it exists.

- *Alienability*: At common law, a fee tail was **not freely alienable**; the grantee could not thwart O's intent that ownership of the property must stay in the grantee's bloodline. What could the grantee, or any other subsequent owner, alienate? At the common law, the owner could only convey the ownership for the rest of his lifetime, i.e., a life estate pur autre vie. Thus, at common law, if O conveyed a fee tail to A, and A subsequently sold his interest in Blackacre to B, B would have owned a life estate pur autre vie (for the life of A). The law did not allow A to keep the fee tail from passing to A's bodily heirs at A's death, even if B was still alive when A died. Today, the owner of the fee tail can **disentail** it—cutting off the rights of his bodily heirs—by conveying a fee to another grantee. In other words, the law allows A to convey a full fee simple even though he only owns a fee tail. If O conveys a fee tail to A, and A subsequently conveys the property "to B in fee simple" or "to B and his heirs," B owns a fee simple absolute, and A has cut off his own bodily heirs, disentailing the fee. This rule only applies to conveyances by deed, not to transfers by will (one cannot disentail a fee tail in one's will). The right of alienability is therefore different under modern law than it was at common law, but the rule for devisability remains the same.

Only a few states today continue to recognize the fee tail, which is widely considered to be a dated vestige of feudal England. Most states have abolished it by statute. In Chapter 9, we will study in detail how grants that would have created a fee tail are handled in the states that have abolished it.

C. FUTURE INTERESTS FOLLOWING EXPIRABLE ESTATES (LIFE ESTATE AND FEE TAIL)

Consider again the example of a lease that will expire in one year. The landlord retains the right to possess the property once the lease expires, because he retained whatever rights he did not convey.

The life estate and fee tail likewise are both expirable. The life estate expires when the person whose life measures it dies, and the fee tail expires when the owner's bloodline runs out. Who owns the property at the expiration of one of these estates? There are two future interests that can immediately and sequentially follow an expirable estate—one is retained by the grantor (a **reversion**), and the other is conveyed by the grantor to a third party (a **remainder**). Before looking at each, it is important to understand that both future interests follow an expirable estate (life estate or fee tail) *immediately at expiration*. In other words, when the life estate or fee tail expires, the future interest immediately becomes the present/possessory estate. These future interests thus wait patiently for the estate to expire and do not cut the expirable estate off, and they step in immediately at expiration; there is no time gap between the expirable estate and these future interests.

---

[2] The only limited exception is if A owns a fee tail and conveys a life estate to B, and B dies before A; then B can devise his interest to his devisee, but only as a life estate pur autre vie for the rest of A's life. At A's death, the property must pass in fee tail to A's issue, if any.

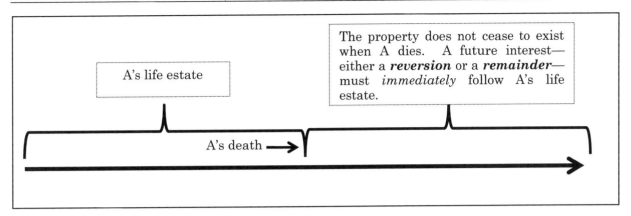

1. REVERSION

When O owns a fee and then conveys a life estate to A and no other interest, O has retained the part of his fee that follows the life estate. A ***reversion*** is the future interest O retains that follows (that is, waits patiently and steps in immediately when the other interest ends) an estate that expires (a life estate or fee tail).[3] O retains a reversion in the following conveyances:

O to A for life (A has a life estate, O has a reversion)

O to A and the heirs of his body (A has a fee tail, O has a reversion)

A reversion is ***alienable, inheritable, and devisable***. Thus, O can sell it or leave it to someone in his will. If O does neither, O's heir will get the reversion at O's death.

2. REMAINDER

A future interest that O conveys to *another party* that immediately follows an expirable estate is a ***remainder***. In other words, rather than retaining a reversion, O conveys to another grantee in the same grant the right to own the property after the expirable estate ends. For example:

> The *grantor* owns a reversion, while a *grantee* owns a remainder.

O to A for life, then to B and his heirs

A has a life estate, and B has a remainder (in fee simple). B owns a property interest that enables him to take possession at the expiration of A's life estate (at A's death). Similarly,

O to A and the heirs of his body, then to B and his heirs

A has a fee tail, and B has a remainder (in fee simple). B will own the property in fee if and when A's fee tail expires (when A's bloodline runs out and thus A has no living bodily heir).

Note that "then" in the above conveyances means ***immediately*** following the preceding estate. "Then" indicates both that B's future interest waits for A's present estate to expire, and thus does not cut it off, and that B's interest instantaneously takes possession when A's interest expires (at A's death if A owns a life estate or when A's bloodline runs out if A has a fee tail).

Can you see why B does not have a remainder in the following examples?

O to A for life, then one year later to B and his heirs

There is a gap between A's and B's interests, so this is not a remainder.

O to A for life, then to B if B gives a proper burial for A

There is a gap, because it is not possible for A to be given a proper burial instantaneously at A's death. This cannot be a remainder.

---

[3] We will later see other instances when O retains a reversion; for now, our focus is solely on a reversion immediately following an expirable estate.

O to A for life, but if A marries X, at that time to B and his heirs

B's interest *cuts off*, rather than patiently follows, A's life estate, so this is not a remainder.[4]

D. FULLY ASSESSING TITLE

Whenever you assess the state of the title, all the interests you identify must add up to a fee simple. If the last interest you identify is not in fee, you have not fully assessed all the parts that O conveyed of his original fee. This full assessment is sometimes referred to as the "quantum" of title. To provide a simple example:

O to A for life

Clearly, on the face of the grant, A has a life estate. Is that quantum? No, because someone has to take possession in fee after A dies. As we learned above, because O owned a fee, he retains whatever he did not convey, which here would be a reversion following the life estate. The life estate plus the reversion fully account for O's original fee (life estate + reversion = fee).

Here is a slightly more difficult example:

O to A for life, then to B for life

On the face of the grant, A has a life estate, and B has a remainder in a life estate. This is not quantum, because the last interest is for life only, not in fee. Again, O retains a reversion when the last interest he conveys is for life. A's life estate, B's remainder for life, and O's reversion combined fully account for O's original fee simple.

E. CLASSIFYING REMAINDERS BY THE
PRESENT ESTATE THEY WILL BECOME

Because remainders are potential present estates, they must be characterized according to the present estate they will ripen into; e.g., a remainder in a life estate, fee tail, or fee simple. For example:

O to A for life, then to B for life

A has a life estate, B has a remainder in a life estate, and O has retained a reversion[5] (following both interests).

O to A for life, then to B and the heirs of his body

A has a life estate, B has a remainder in fee tail, and O has retained a reversion.

O to A for life, then to B and his heirs

A has a life estate, and B has a remainder in fee. O has fully conveyed his fee and thus has not retained a reversion here.

---

[4] In Chapter 6, you will learn what interest B has in each of these three examples (spoiler alert—it is an "executory interest"). Like a remainder, you need to wait patiently for this concept to unfold.

[5] A reversion is presumed to be in fee simple absolute unless stated otherwise. We will learn in Chapter 6 when O retains a reversion that is not in fee simple absolute.

CHAPTER 2 SUMMARY

Present Estate: A property interest that entitles the owner to the present use and possession of the property.

Future Interest: A property interest that the owner presently owns but where the right of use and possession is delayed until a future time.

Fee Simple Absolute: The ultimate interest in realty, or "full" title.

Life Estate: An estate that lasts only for the duration of the grantee's life.

Life Estate Pur Autre Vie: A life estate measured by the life of someone other than the grantee.

Fee Tail: An estate that passes linearly through the grantee's bloodline ("issue").

Disentail: A fee tail is disentailed when the owner presently conveys by deed a fee simple absolute to a grantee.

Reversion: A future interest held by the grantor that, among other things, immediately follows an expirable estate.

Remainder: A future interest, held by a grantee, that immediately follows an expirable estate (a life estate or a fee tail).

Your assessment of the state of the title must fully account for all of the original grantor's fee simple (quantum).

F. PRACTICE PROBLEMS

For problems 1–4, identify which attributes of property rights are associated with each property interest (*the next chapter will provide more information on the attributes of a remainder*).

    1. Fee simple absolute

    2. Life estate

    3. Fee tail

    4. Reversion

Answer problem 5.

    5. Name the expirable estates and the two types of future interests that patiently follow them.

For problems 6–10, read the conveyance, identify the words of purchase, the words of limitation, and the present estate granted to A (remember, O is presumed to own a fee simple absolute).

   6.   O conveys Blackacre "to A and his heirs."

   7.   O conveys Blackacre "to A and his bodily heirs."

   8.   O conveys Blackacre "to A for life."

   9.   O conveys Blackacre "to A."

   10. O conveys Blackacre "to A for the life of B."

For problems 11–18, read the conveyance and determine whether—if at all—A's estate is followed by a reversion or a remainder.

   11. O to A for life.

   12. O to A and his bodily heirs, then to B.

   13. O to A and his heirs.

   14. O to A and his bodily heirs, then after one year to B.

   15. O to A in fee tail.

   16. O to A for life, then to B.

   17. O to A, but if A starts smoking, then at that time to B.

18. O to A in fee tail. A subsequently conveys "to B in fee."

For problems 19–21, read the conveyance or series of conveyances and identify the state of title (i.e., list all of the property interests and who owns them). If there is a series of conveyances or events, identify the state of title after each conveyance or event.

19. O conveys Greenacre to A and his bodily heirs. A then devises Greenacre to his best friend, B, and his heirs. A has no bodily heirs at his death.

20. A executes a will devising Blackacre, which he does not yet own, to B for life, then to C in fee. O then conveys Blackacre to A. A then dies.

21. O conveys Blackacre to A in fee simple, then to B for life.

G. CLASS DISCUSSION PROBLEMS

For problems 1–15, read the conveyance or series of conveyances and identify the state of the title (i.e., list all of the property interests and who owns them). If there is a series of conveyances or events, identify the state of the title after each conveyance or event.

1. O to A for life.

2. O to A in fee simple absolute.

3. O to A in fee tail.

4. O to A in fee tail, then to B and his heirs.

5. O to A for life, then to B and the female heirs of her body.

6. O to A for the life of B, then to C for life.

7. O conveys Blackacre to A and his bodily heirs. Later, A finalizes the following conveyance: "A to B in fee simple absolute."

8. O conveys Blackacre to A for life. Later, A conveys Blackacre to B in fee simple absolute.

9. O conveys Blackacre to A in fee simple absolute. Later, A finalizes the following conveyance: "A to B for the life of A."

10. T executes his will, which states, "I, T, devise Blackacre to A in fee simple absolute." T is still alive.

11. T executes a will, devising Blackacre to A in fee simple absolute. T dies.

12. O to A for life, then to B for life, then to C in fee tail.

13. In one conveyance, O grants Blackacre to A for life. In a later conveyance, O grants his future rights in Blackacre (i.e., the rights to Blackacre after A dies) to B.

14. O conveys Mapleacre to A for life, then to B and his heirs. O later convinces B to convey "all my interest in Mapleacre" back to O.

15. O conveys Blackacre to A for life, then to B for life, then to C and his bodily heirs, then to D for life, then to E for life. B dies, then D dies, then A dies, and then C dies. C dies without a bodily heir.

Answer problem 16.

16. Suppose you are a practicing attorney, and a client asks you to draft a conveyance. Your client, an elderly widow, owns Whiteacre, a 100 acre estate, and she wants to give Whiteacre to her only daughter, Anne. However, your client wants to control who owns Whiteacre after her daughter dies. After her daughter's death, your client wants her grandson—Bob—to own Whiteacre. How should you draft the conveyance?

CHAPTER 3

FURTHER CLASSIFYING REMAINDERS; DESTRUCTIBILITY

■ ■ ■

In Chapter 2, you learned that a remainder follows an expirable estate (life estate or fee tail) immediately at expiration. You also learned that a remainder must be further classified according to the present estate it will become. We now turn to another important attribute of remainders—whether they are classified as vested or contingent.

A. VESTED REMAINDERS

The distinction between a vested and a contingent remainder is based on whether or not the remainder meets the criteria for being vested; if the remainder does not, it is contingent by default. For a remainder to be vested, two requirements must **_both_** be met:

- *There must be no "condition precedent"*—besides the expiration of the prior estate, there cannot be a condition that must be fulfilled in order for the remainder to become a present estate (become possessory) when the expirable estate ends;

and

- *The owner of the remainder must be ascertainable*—you must be able to specify that the owner is currently born, or in existence if an entity, and identifiable.

Let's consider each of these attributes separately:

"No condition precedent." Because a remainder immediately follows an expirable estate, every remainder by definition is subject to the expiration of that preceding estate (life estate or fee tail). For a remainder to be vested, it cannot be subject to a condition precedent other than the expiration of the preceding estate. A condition precedent is a condition that either precedes, or is directly attached to, the remainder. Punctuation is the key to determining whether a condition that affects a remainder is a condition precedent.

> A condition precedent either comes before, or is directly attached to, the remainder.

Here are two grants containing a condition precedent:

> *O to A for life, then to B and his heirs if B does not marry*
>
> *O to A for life, then if B does not marry, to B and his heirs*

The first example includes a condition that is directly attached to the remainder (in other words, there is no punctuation between the remainder and the condition). The second example involves a condition that comes before the remainder. Both examples include a condition that must be met before the remainder can become a present estate. Both involve conditions precedent, and, assuming B is not yet married, neither remainder is vested because the condition has not yet been satisfied.

"Ascertainable owner." The second requirement for vesting is the owner of the remainder must be ascertainable. Compare these two conveyances:

O to A for life, then to B

"B" is a name, like John Doe. A named person has presumably already been born and is thus ascertainable. Compare this remainder:

O to A for life, then to the first-born child of B

Unless B has a first-born child at the time of the grant, the owner of this remainder is not yet born and thus is not ascertainable. (You would say that "B's first-born child" owns the remainder.) Because both requirements must be met for the remainder to be vested, this remainder is contingent.

A remainder to a class is vested if any one person is born and ascertainable; this is called a **vested remainder "subject to open."**[1] For example, consider this conveyance:

> A remainder to a class is vested subject to open if any one person in the class is ascertained and there is no unmet condition precedent.

O to A for life, then to the children of B in fee simple

If at the time of the grant B has one child, X, then X is a born and ascertainable owner. There is no condition precedent attached to the remainder. This remainder is vested. It is, however, "subject to open," because other children of B could be born later and share ownership of the remainder interest with X.[2]

By contrast, consider this example:

O to A for life, then to the children of B who reach 21

Assume that at the time this grant is made, B has one child, X, who is 3. Here, the class of owners is not just the children of B, but the children of B who reach 21. X is a child of B but X has not yet reached 21; X is therefore not an "ascertainable" person in that X does not yet meet the definition of ownership. This remainder is not vested, and X does not yet own it; X will not own it (be an "ascertainable owner") unless and until X is 21 years old.

Vested remainders are alienable, devisable, and inheritable, **if** they still exist. For example, if B owns a vested remainder in a life estate, B cannot leave the remainder by will or intestacy because the interest will expire at B's death, and thus, by definition, B will have nothing to leave to a devisee or heir.

B. CONTINGENT REMAINDERS

A contingent remainder is simply a non-vested remainder, a remainder that does not meet both criteria for vesting. Consider the following examples:

O to A for life, then if B has not married C, to B and his heirs

In order for B to obtain title after A dies, B must not have married C. If B has married C at the time of the grant, he will obviously never get possession of the property. If, at the time of the grant, B has not married C, this condition precedent must be satisfied (or perhaps it would be more accurate to say not violated) by A's death for B's remainder to vest. This is a condition

---

[1] This remainder is also sometimes called vested "subject to partial divestment." This book will only use "subject to open," but you should be aware of the other label because you may run across it in other sources. Later, we will study a way a vested remainder might be "subject to divestment"; this is only tangentially related. Be careful not to confuse these concepts.

[2] You may wonder what the state of the title will be when B dies if B has had another child. Two or more people owning the same present estate, such as a fee simple, at the same time is a **concurrent estate**. You will study concurrent estates later in your Property course.

precedent rather than a definition of the class of ownership (e.g., "the children of B who reach 21"). B therefore owns a contingent remainder in fee following A's life estate.[3]

O to A for life, then to the first-born son of Q

If Q has not had a son, this remainder is contingent because the owner is not born and thus is not ascertainable.

O to A for life, then to the children of B who reach 21

If at the time of this grant B has only one child, X, who is 3, this remainder is contingent because the owner is not yet ascertainable; no child of B has yet reached 21. It is not vested subject to open because X does not meet the criteria for ownership (a child of B who has reached 21). Therefore, "the children of B who reach 21" own a contingent remainder in fee. If X later reaches 21, then X would be an ascertainable owner, and the remainder would become vested subject to open (there is no condition precedent connected to this remainder).

O to A for life, then to B and his heirs if B has married C

Remember that remainders *always* wait patiently until the previous estate expires. If B marries C while A is alive, then the condition precedent is met and the remainder vests. But B must still wait for A to die before B's vested remainder becomes possessory.

The last two examples also illustrate that contingent remainders do not necessarily remain contingent. Once the owner can be ascertained and any condition precedent has been met, the contingent remainder vests, even if it is not yet possessory.

Contingent remainders were not alienable at common law but are under modern law. They are devisable and inheritable, if they still exist (e.g., if B owns a contingent remainder for life following A's life estate, and if B dies before A, his interest expires at his death and thus he has nothing left to leave to his devisee or heir).

C. ALTERNATIVE CONTINGENT REMAINDERS

A contingent remainder can be followed by an alternative contingent remainder, in the event the first remainder does not vest. Consider this example:

O to A for life, then if B has married C, to B and his heirs, otherwise to D and his heirs

If B has not married C at the time O makes this grant, B's remainder is contingent because it is subject to a condition precedent (B has to marry C by the time A dies—"if B *has* married C"). D's remainder conversely is contingent on B *not* marrying C by the time A dies, and thus D's remainder is also subject to a condition precedent. D's remainder is an *alternative* in the event B's does not vest. A owns a life estate, B owns a contingent remainder in fee, and D owns an alternative contingent remainder in fee. As we shall now see, however, this is not quantum; O has also retained a reversion.

D. REVERSION FOLLOWING A CONTINGENT REMAINDER

A contingent remainder that is the last interest conveyed is always followed by a reversion retained by the grantor. By definition a contingent remainder is uncertain; it must vest for its owner to possess the property in the future. For example:

---

[3]   By its express terms, this condition only affects B's interest before it becomes a present estate ("then if B <u>has not</u> <u>married</u> C"). In Chapter 5, we will encounter other types of conditions that affect present (possessory) estates. Regardless, a condition precedent *never* encumbers an already possessory estate. A condition precedent only determines whether the remainder can vest and thus whether it can subsequently become possessory.

O to A for life, then to B if B has graduated law school

What happens if B does not graduate law school by the time A dies? Because O did not specify that anyone else would get the property if this condition is not satisfied (there is no alternative contingent remainder), O by definition retained that right, which was part of his original fee. O has retained a reversion following A's life estate and B's contingent remainder in fee.

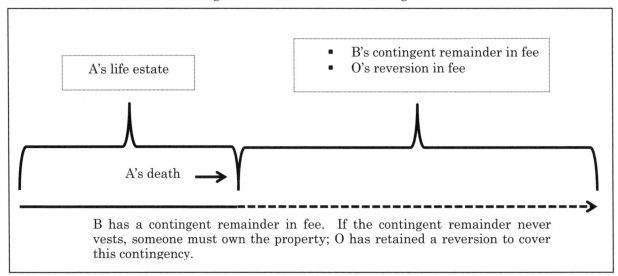

Let's return to previous examples of contingent remainders:

O to A for life, then to the first-born son of Q

If Q has no son at the time of the grant, this remainder is contingent because the owner is not born and ascertainable. A owns a life estate, "the first-born son of Q" owns a contingent remainder in fee, and O has retained a reversion.

O to A for life, then to the children of B who reach 21

A owns a life estate. If at the time of the grant B has one child, X, who is 3, the remainder is contingent and owned by an as yet unascertainable person (no child of B is yet 21). "The children of B who reach 21" therefore own a contingent remainder in fee, and O has retained a reversion.

O to A for life, then if B has not married C, to B and his heirs

A owns a life estate. If B has not yet married C, B owns a contingent remainder in fee, and O has retained a reversion.

Reconsider this example from earlier in this chapter:

O to A for life, then to B if B has graduated law school

O retained a reversion to account for the possibility that B might not graduate law school. But what if O also conveys an alternative contingent remainder to C?

O to A for life, then to B if B has graduated law school, otherwise to C

At first glance, it appears O conveyed everything he had; either B or C will own Blackacre when A dies. But as we will now learn, O still retains a reversion, because contingent remainders can be destroyed by operation of law in certain circumstances.

E. DESTRUCTIBILITY OF CONTINGENT REMAINDERS

At common law, contingent remainders were vulnerable—they could be destroyed automatically as a matter of law if they did not vest before or at the expiration of the preceding estate or before certain events occurred. This is the doctrine of **destructibility of contingent remainders**. Because of the doctrine of destructibility, O retains a reversion whenever the last interest conveyed is a contingent remainder. If the remainder is destroyed, the property will revert to O when the expirable estate ends.

There are three circumstances under which a contingent remainder can be destroyed:

1. Destruction for Failure to Vest by the Expiration of the Preceding Estate

When an expirable estate ends, the **next non-contingent interest takes possession** (becomes the present estate). What is a "non-contingent" interest? Either a reversion or a vested remainder. Under the common law destructibility rule, **a contingent remainder is destroyed if it does not vest before or at the expiration of the preceding estate**. Returning to an example from above:

> Only contingent remainders can be destroyed in the following ways. Vested remainders and other future interests you will learn about later are not destructible.

O to A for life, then if B has turned 21, to B and his heirs

A owns a life estate. If B is not 21 at the time of the grant, B owns a contingent remainder in fee, and O has retained a reversion. If A dies before B is 21, B's interest will be destroyed for not vesting prior to or at the expiration of A's life estate. Under the common law destructibility rule, B must meet the condition of turning 21 before or at A's death or his remainder is destroyed, never to return—you do not wait to see if B turns 21 sometime after A's death. This also illustrates that the remainder must **immediately** follow an expirable estate—there can be no gap to wait for B to turn 21 later.[4]

Consider this example:

O to A for life, then to B and his heirs if B survives A

A owns a life estate, B owns a contingent remainder in fee, and O has retained a reversion. B's contingent remainder is an example of one that can vest immediately at the expiration of A's life estate. If B dies before A, B's remainder will never vest and thus will cease to exist. If A dies before B, then B's remainder will both vest and become possessory immediately at A's death.

Compare this example:

O to A for life, then to B if B marries C, otherwise to D (B has not married C)

Again, A owns a life estate, B owns a contingent remainder in fee, D owns an alternative contingent remainder in fee, and O has retained a reversion. Here, the grant does not expressly require the condition to be met by A's death. What if A dies, B and C are still alive, and B has not yet married C? A's life estate expires, and the next non-contingent interest must take possession. Clearly, B's remainder has not vested and thus is destroyed. What about D's remainder? Because B and C could still marry, the condition precedent to D's remainder—that B never marry C—has also not been met. D's remainder has therefore not vested and is also destroyed, and title reverts to O. If B and C never married but B or C (let's say B) died before A died, then D's remainder vested at B's death, because B will never marry C. D thus in that instance would own the property in fee when A dies.

2. Destruction by Merger

A contingent remainder can also be destroyed by **merger**, the combination of an expirable estate and either a reversion or vested remainder in fee (i.e., life estate/fee tail + reversion/vested remainder in fee = fee). For example:

---

[4] We will learn in Chapter 8 that this common law rule is not universally applied today. Again, wait patiently for this to unfold in due time.

O to A for life, then to B and his heirs if B marries C (B has not married C)

The state of the title is A owns a life estate, B owns a contingent remainder in fee, and O has retained a reversion. If O conveys his reversion to A, or if A conveys his life estate to O, the two interests (life estate + reversion) are now owned by the same person, and they merge into a fee (life estate + reversion = fee), destroying B's interest.

To illustrate further why the merged interests equal a fee, consider this simple example:

O to A for life

A owns a life estate and O has retained a reversion. Combined, those two interests fully account for what was O's fee. If O would convey his reversion to A, A would now own a life estate and a reversion. These two interests combined fully account for the title O originally had and thus are viewed as merging into a fee (life estate + reversion = fee).

Likewise, returning to our more complex example:

O to A for life, then to B and his heirs if B marries C (B has not married C)

When A's original life estate and O's reversion are both owned by either A or O, the law views the two interests as equivalent to a fee (life estate + reversion = fee). If B's remainder is still contingent because B has not yet married C, the remainder is destroyed by merger. The life estate and reversion combine into a fee, and it is not possible to have an interest in addition to a fee—a fee is full title, all there is or can be. By contrast, if B had married C previously, B's remainder would have vested, O's reversion would have disappeared, and B could not lose his interest through merger (indeed, because O no longer owns a reversion, there would be nothing left to merge with the life estate).

Consider this example:

O to A and the heirs of his body, then to B and his heirs if B marries C (B has not married C)

A owns a fee tail, B owns a contingent remainder in fee, and O has retained a reversion. If O then conveys his reversion to A, A now has a fee (fee tail + reversion = fee) and B's interest is destroyed. (O apparently changed his mind regarding whether the property should stay in A's bloodline.) What if instead A conveys his life interest back to O? O now owns a life estate (pur autre vie for the life of A) <u>and</u> a reversion, which likewise combine to equal a fee. Not only is B's contingent remainder destroyed, but the property will no longer go to A's bodily heirs at A's death. (This result is similar to the concept of disentailing a fee tail that we learned in Chapter 2.)

<u>The "more than one grant" rule for destruction by merger</u>: A contingent remainder can only be destroyed when the merged interests are conveyed in more than one grant; the destruction by merger rule does not apply to interests created *only* in the initial grant. For example:

O to A for life, then if B marries C, to B for life, then to A and his heirs

You may think that A's life estate should merge with his vested remainder in fee[5] to create a fee and destroy B's contingent remainder, but destructibility by merger does **not** apply to interests granted to the same owner in the original conveyance. However, if A *later* conveys his life estate **and** his vested remainder in fee to someone else (e.g., X), and B has not yet married C, then the two interests merge, X owns the property in fee, and B's contingent remainder is destroyed. If B married C before A conveys all of his interest in the property to X, then B's

---

[5] You also may wonder how A can own a remainder in fee that follows A's life estate; in other words, how can A own an interest that will become possessory only *after* his or her death? Remember that vested remainders are inheritable and devisable. Upon A's death, A's vested remainder in fee becomes part of A's estate, and it is either devised by will or inherited by A's heir. A owns this remainder but of course will not be able to enjoy possession of it given that it will become a present estate only after A's life estate expires (after A dies). This is an example of how a future interest gives the owner a present title but not the present right of possession.

remainder vested and cannot be destroyed. This would leave the state of the title as X owning a life estate pur autre vie for the life of A, B owning a vested remainder for life, and X owning a vested remainder in fee. Remember, *only contingent remainders are destructible*.

3. *Destruction by Renunciation*

Contingent remainders can also be destroyed by the **renunciation** of the preceding estate, which occurs when the present estate owner declares he no longer wants his property interest and thus essentially abandons it. If an expirable estate is revoked or renounced, a contingent remainder immediately following it is destroyed.[6] For example:

O to A for life, then to B if B marries C (B has not married C)

A owns a life estate, B owns a contingent remainder in fee, and O has retained a reversion. If A renounces his life estate, the next non-contingent (i.e., vested) interest takes possession. If B has not married C, the next non-contingent interest is O's reversion, which becomes possessory in fee, destroying B's remainder. The renunciation of the preceding estate thus cuts short the opportunity for B's contingent remainder to vest. Once destroyed, the contingent remainder is gone for good, so in this instance, it would be irrelevant whether, after destruction, B marries C.

Consider this example:

O to A for life, then to B if B has married C, otherwise to D
(B has not married C)

A owns a life estate, B owns a contingent remainder in fee, and D owns an alternative contingent remainder in fee. It may appear that either B or D is certain to take possession at A's death and thus that O did not retain a reversion. However, *a contingency cannot be finally tested until the <u>natural</u> expiration of the preceding estate*. If A renounces his life estate before B has married C, neither contingent remainder has vested yet, because the contingency cannot be finally tested until A dies. B has not married C and thus B's remainder has not vested; and yet because A has not died, B has not yet violated the condition—by not marrying C *by A's death*—and so D's remainder is not vested either. Because A's life estate is gone due to renunciation, the next non-contingent interest must take possession. Neither remainder has vested, so the next non-contingent interest is O's reversion; title therefore reverts to O, who implicitly retained a reversion to cover this very possibility. Because O takes the property in fee, both remainders are destroyed. This is an example of why a reversion must be included after alternative contingent remainders, even if it looks like the full fee has been conveyed without the reversion.

F. ONE FINAL COMPLEXITY

Consider this conveyance:

O to A for life, then to B for life if B ever starts a bee farm, then to C

A owns a life estate, followed by B's remainder. If B has not yet started a bee farm, B's remainder is a contingent remainder in life estate (contingent because of an unfulfilled condition precedent). Is C's interest a remainder? Yes, because "then" signifies "immediately next," and the interest follows a life interest. Is C's remainder vested or contingent? Read the language of this conveyance carefully. C's remainder is not introduced by "otherwise" or by a phrase like "but if B does not start a bee farm." **C's remainder is not contingent simply because it follows a contingent remainder.** Instead, it appears that C is guaranteed to get the property after both A's and B's interests are gone (at the latest, after both have died and their life estates have expired). Thus, whether or not B launches a bee farm, C's remainder is

---

[6] Under English common law, a contingent remainder could also be destroyed by forfeiture (as a penalty for certain offenses, including conveying a greater title than one owned). American courts have generally not applied this form of destruction and thus it will not be addressed further in this book.

vested, and C will eventually own the property in fee. The interest O conveyed to C is thus what would have been O's reversion following B's interest. In other words, if B never starts a bee farm, C will take possession at A's death. If B does start a bee farm, C will take possession after both A and B have died and thus both of their life estates have expired.

CHAPTER 3 SUMMARY

A remainder is vested if:

    1) There is no condition precedent, <u>and</u>

    2) The owner is born and ascertainable (thus ascertained).

Otherwise, the remainder is contingent.

Condition Precedent: A condition that is either directly attached to, or before, the remainder.

Contingent remainders that are the last interest conveyed are always followed by reversions.

Under the common law, contingent remainders are destructible for three reasons:

    1) Failure to vest by the expiration of the preceding estate,

    2) Merger, or

    3) Renunciation.

G. PRACTICE PROBLEMS

For problems 1–2, identify which attributes of property rights are associated with each property interest.

    1. Vested remainder

    2. Contingent remainder

Answer problems 3–5.

    3. What are the characteristics of a vested remainder?

    4. Under the common law, what are the three ways in which a contingent remainder can be destroyed?

    5. What interests do reversions follow?

For problems 6–16, identify if there is a remainder and, if so, whether it is vested, contingent, or vested subject to open. Further classify any remainder by what present estate it will be when it becomes possessory (e.g., fee, fee tail, or life estate).

    6. O to A for life, then to B for life.

7. O to A for life, then to B's children in fee simple (B does not yet have any children).

8. O to A for life, then to B's children in fee simple (B's first child was born yesterday).

9. O to A in fee simple absolute, but if A ever raises pigs on the land, then to B.

10. O to A and the heirs of his body, then if B buys a Ferrari, to B and his heirs (B has not bought a Ferrari).

11. O to A in fee tail, then to B if B buys a Ferrari (B just bought a Ferrari).

12. O to A for life, then to A's children who reach age 21 *if* they have graduated high school. Consider the following alternative fact patterns:

    a. A has one child, B, who is 17. B is a junior in high school.

    b. A has one child, B, who is 19. B graduated high school.

    c. A has one child, B, who just turned 21. B graduated high school.

    d. A has two children, B and C. B is 23, and he just graduated high school. C just turned 21, and he already graduated high school.

    e. A has one child, B, who is 21 and has a GED.

13. O to A in fee tail, then to B in fee tail.

14. O to A for life, then to B if B cares for A when A is infirm and over the age of 75 (A is younger than 75).

15. O to A for life, then to B if B marries C, otherwise to D (B has not yet married C).

16. O to A for life.

For problems 17–20, assume that your jurisdiction follows the common law rule of destructibility of contingent remainders. Determine whether the series of events causes any contingent remainders to be destroyed, and who owns the property once the events are completed.

17. O grants Blackacre to A for life, then if B has joined the military, to B in fee. Five years after the conveyance, A dies, and B has not yet joined the military (B is only 10 years old when A dies).

18. O grants Blackacre to A for life, then to B's children who reach age 21 for life, then to C. B has two children, D (who is 18) and E (who is 15). One month later, A conveys his entire interest in Blackacre to C.

19. O grants Blackacre to A for life, then to B for life if B marries C, then to A in fee. At a later time, A conveys his entire interest in Blackacre to D.

    a. In addition, when A conveys his interests to D, B has not yet married C.

    b. In contrast to the prior example, B does marry C before A conveys his interests to D.

20. O grants Blackacre to A and the heirs of his body, then to B for life. At a later time, A conveys a life estate pur autre vie to O.

For problems 21–24, identify the state of title. If events are described after the conveyance, give the state of title at each stage in the process (i.e., at the time of the conveyance, after the first event, and so on). Assume that the common law rule of destructibility applies.

21. T devises Blackacre to A for life, then to B for life if B becomes a pediatrician (T just died, and B is already a pediatrician).

22. T devises Blackacre to A for life, then to T's children who reach age 20 (T, who just died, has three children, B, C, and D, but only B has reached 20). Tragically, all of T's children die in a car accident leaving T's funeral, and C and D were still not 20. A dies ten years later.

23. O grants Blackacre to A for life, then to O's children if they all reach age 20 (O has three children, B, C, and D, but only B has reached age 20). A few years later, C turns 20. The day before D turns 20, B—a pilot—takes his siblings for a flight in his Cessna. B crashes just after takeoff and none of the siblings survive.

24. O grants Blackacre to A in fee tail, then to B's children for the duration of B's life (B has no children). A dies three years later, leaving no issue besides his one daughter—C—behind. One year after A's death, B has a boy—D. Then, in another fifteen years, B dies, followed shortly thereafter by C's death (C has no issue).

H. CLASS DISCUSSION PROBLEMS

For problems 1–13, identify the state of title. If events are described after the conveyance, give the state of title at each stage in the process (i.e., at the time of the conveyance, after the first event, and so on). Assume that the common law rule of destructibility applies.

1. O grants Blackacre to A for life, then to B.

2. O grants Blackacre to A for life, then to B in fee tail.

3. O grants Blackacre to A for life, then to B for life.

4. O grants Blackacre to A in fee tail, then to B's children (B does not have any children).

5. O grants Blackacre to A for life, then if B has children, to B (B does not yet have any children). Later, A dies and B still has no children.

6. O grants Blackacre to A for life, then to B if B has had children (B has two children). Later, A dies.

7. O grants Blackacre to A for life, then to B if B then has children, otherwise to C (B does not yet have children). Later, A dies and B still has no children.

8. O grants Blackacre to A in fee tail, then to B for life if B starts a charity (B has not yet started a charity). Two years later, A dies without issue but B never started a charity.

9. O grants Blackacre to A in fee tail, then to B's grandchildren born in the 20 years following this conveyance. One year later, C—a granddaughter of B—is born. Another year later, D—a grandson of B—is born.

10. O conveys Blackacre to A for life, then to B for life if B becomes a chemical engineer (O just died, and B is not a chemical engineer). O devises his remaining interest in Blackacre to C. The day after O's death, A conveys his entire interest in Blackacre to C.

11. O grants Blackacre to A and his bodily heirs, then to B if B goes on a mission trip to India (B has never been to India).

    a. Twenty years later, A dies; B still has never been on a mission trip to India (A is only survived by one daughter, C).

    b. Five years after A dies, C dies without issue. As of C's death, B has never traveled to India.

12. O grants Blackacre to A for life, then to B for life, then if C has successfully climbed Mt. Everest, to C, otherwise to D. Thirty years later, both A and B die. C has not climbed Mt. Everest.

13. In practice, you will find that conveyances are often ambiguous and poorly drafted. Consider this: "I, Orville, hereby convey Silveracre to my sister Allison for life. Then, because I am sure my niece Betty will care for her mother, Allison, in her old age, to Betty for life. Finally, Silveracre will go to Betty's daughter, Clara, and her heirs." Twenty years later, Allison turns eighty and her health begins deteriorating. Although Allison and Betty have drifted apart, Allison remains close to her granddaughter Clara, who moves in at Silveracre to care for Allison. Allison thanks Clara by granting her "all my interest in Silveracre." Allison dies a few

years later, and Clara visits your law office because her mother, Betty, is demanding that she vacate Silveracre. What advice should you give?

Problem 14 contains a pair of conveyances and a series of subsequent factual developments. For both grants, analyze the state of the title at the time of the grant and then at each point in the chronological chain.

14. O grants Whiteacre to A for life, then if B has married C, to B.

O grants Whiteacre to A for his lifetime, then to B if B is married to C.

    a. At the time of the grant, B and C are not married, and A is still alive.

    b. Two years later B and C marry. A is still alive.

    c. Thirty years after marrying B, C dies. A is still alive.

    d. One year after C dies, A dies.

CHAPTER 4

TWO ADDITIONAL COMMON LAW RULES LIMITING REMAINDERS

■ ■ ■

In addition to destructibility, the common law included two other rules that restricted contingent remainders, regardless of the grantor's intent, and had the effect of clearing title to the property.

A. THE RULE IN SHELLEY'S CASE

The Rule in Shelley's Case is a common law rule that applies by law at the time of the grant, notwithstanding O's contrary intent. The rule is very straightforward: ***The grantor cannot convey an interest in a life estate[1] to a grantee and, in the same grant, convey a remainder to that same grantee's heirs. If the grantor does so, as a matter of law, the grantee owns the remainder conveyed to his heirs.***

> In future chapters you will learn about another interest that the grantor could convey to the grantee's heirs. However, the Rule in Shelley's Case *only* applies to remainders.

It is easier to see the Rule in operation than to memorize or state it. Here is an example of a conveyance that violates the Rule in Shelley's Case:

O to A for life, then to A's heirs

In this example, the grant on its face conveys a life estate to A and a remainder to A's heirs. The remainder is contingent because A's heir(s) cannot be ascertained until A dies. O therefore retained a reversion. However, the Rule in Shelley's Case mandates as a matter of law that the remainder to A's heirs is owned by A. In effect, the Rule rewords the conveyance to say:

O to A for life, then to A and his heirs

A thus owns both a life estate and a vested remainder in fee, which leaves A with a fee simple by merger (life estate + vested remainder in fee = fee), and O no longer has a reversion.[2] Notice the effect this rule has on the state of the title. If the original conveyance stood, the title would be divided among three interest holders, one of whom, A's heir, is not unascertainable. By contrast, the Rule in Shelley's Case clears title so that it is held by one person, A, in fee.

The Rule in Shelley's Case also applies when the grantee receives a life estate pur autre vie. For example:

O to A for the life of B, then to A's heirs

The Rule invalidates the remainder to A's heirs, leaving it to A in fee instead, and thus rewording the grant to read:

---

[1] At common law, the Rule in Shelley's Case also applied when the grantee's interest was in fee tail. However, because most jurisdictions do not recognize the fee tail, with regard to the Rule in Shelley's case, "in the American cases the freehold is invariably a life estate." KURTZ, MOYNIHAN'S INTRODUCTION TO THE LAW OF REAL PROPERTY 192 (4th ed. 2005). This book will therefore apply the Rule only where the interest conveyed to the grantee is in a life estate.

[2] You may recall that we previously learned not to merge interests conveyed in the original grant, but that rule only prohibited merging original interests ***to destroy a contingent remainder***. Here, the ***merger*** does not destroy a contingent remainder; the Rule in Shelley's Case already did so.

O to A for the life of B, then to A and his heirs

A now owns a life estate pur autre vie and a vested remainder in fee, leaving A with a fee by merger.

Consider another grant to which the Rule in Shelley's Case applies:

O to A for life, then to B for life, then to B's heirs

A owns a life estate. On the face of the grant, B owns a vested remainder in a life estate, which is followed by a contingent remainder in fee owned by B's heirs (contingent because the owner is not ascertainable until B dies), with O retaining a reversion because the last interest is a contingent remainder. The Rule in Shelley's Case applies because an interest in a life estate, here B's vested remainder for life, cannot be conveyed to a grantee with a remainder in that grantee's heirs created in the same grant. The Rule requires, as a matter of law, that the interest to B's heirs be treated as if it had been conveyed to B, rewording the conveyance by operation of law to say this:

O to A for life, then to B for life, then to B and his heirs

A now owns a life estate, and B owns a vested remainder for life and also a vested remainder in fee. O no longer retains a reversion because the last interest is now vested in fee. B's two remainders can merge, revising the grant as follows:

O to A for life, then to B and his heirs

A therefore owns a life estate, and B owns a vested remainder in fee. Although this result is not what O intended, it does help clear title, vesting interests only in ascertainable persons. This is just one example of how the common law tended to apply rigid rules rather than consistently giving effect to the grantor's intent (another is the common law requirement that "and his heirs" was required to convey a fee, and thus a very clear grant—e.g., "to A in fee simple"—would not have sufficed to create a fee).

Today, because modern law generally favors implementing the grantor's intent, most states have abolished the Rule in Shelley's Case, although some still apply it.

B. THE RULE AGAINST PERPETUITIES (RAP)

Don't be overwhelmed by this rule! It is not as complicated as it seems at first glance, at least for the purposes of this book and a typical Property course. If you work hard to master the explanations that follow, including working through all the problems in this book, you can understand and properly apply—even master—the basic principles of the Rule against Perpetuities (RAP).

> The RAP will take time to get used to, but don't get discouraged reading the explanations of the concepts; working through numerous examples will help you master the intricacies of the RAP.

The RAP is a time restriction on dead-hand control of certain future interests. Like the Rule in Shelley's Case, it helps clear title, specifically by eliminating some potentially perpetual, uncertain interests. Here is the traditional phrasing of the rule: ***No interest is good unless it must vest, if at all, within 21 years of a life in being at the creation of the interest.*** The meaning of that statement is not self-evident; it helps to break the RAP down into its component parts and to explain each one:

- "No interest" is very misleading. ***The RAP can invalidate three (and only three) future interests. We will now consider two: contingent remainders and remainders to a class of persons*** (e.g., vested remainders subject to open).[3]

---

[3] We will consider the third, the executory interest, in Chapter 6. Again, like a remainder, you need to wait patiently for this to unfold!

It would be more accurate to label the RAP as the Rule against Some Perpetuities, but we must use the label the common law provided.

- ***Always follow this pattern of analysis:***
  - First analyze the state of the title on the face of the grant;
  - Second, apply any other rules of law that affect the state of the title (e.g., the Rule in Shelley's Case);
  - Third, determine if the resulting state of the title includes one of the future interests that the RAP can invalidate; and
  - Finally, if the grant does include such a future interest, test whether the interest withstands the rule.

As you walk through these steps, keep in mind that you are to be objective; your job is to ***test*** the interests, ***not*** to try to save them. As John Chipman Gray stated in his treatise on the RAP, after you first analyze the title on the face of the grant, "the Rule is to be remorselessly applied."[4] You must apply the RAP strictly and without remorse, letting the chips fall where they may. There are several principles to keep in mind when analyzing how the RAP affects a conveyance:

- An interest that the RAP invalidates is void at creation, which is the time of conveyance for a deed or at the death of the testator for a will.

- A ***life in being*** is any person alive at the time of the grant (or at the testator's death for a will). You should focus on all lives in being—anyone you know was alive at the time the interest was created—but ***most importantly, anyone identified in the grant or devise, including people who are mentioned but receive no property interest*** (e.g., the grantor or the "autre vie" measuring a life estate). Anyone who is conceived at the time an interest is created and later born is considered a life in being for the purposes of testing an interest under the RAP.

  > There are billions of people alive at any point in time. But the conditions in the conveyance—the conditions that determine whether the interest will vest in time—probably involve only people mentioned in the grant. That is why we focus on those people.

- The time restriction of the RAP is the full life of a person alive at the creation of the interest (a "life in being") plus 21 years. In other words, for an interest to be valid, you must be able, at the time of the grant or devise, to identify someone (indeed, anyone) who is then alive and ***guarantee*** that the required event ***must*** occur within 21 years of that person's life (i.e., within 21 years of his death). Twenty-one years may seem arbitrary, but it was considered the measure of a generation; the common law judges wanted to limit the existence of some interests to no more than one generation beyond the generations alive when the interest was created (thus keeping those interests from being potentially perpetual—hence "Against (Some) Perpetuities").

- Don't get thrown by this arbitrary time limit. The common law judges could have required the necessary event to have happened within some set time frame (e.g., within 90 years of the deed or will). Instead, they decided to limit dead-hand control over some future interests to one generation (21 years) beyond the generations alive at the time of the grant. Don't shut down on the rule just because it could have been conceptually easier!

- Only one validating life in being needs to exist in order for the tested interest to survive the RAP. Accordingly, if you can guarantee that the interest will "vest, if at

---

4   GRAY, THE RULE AGAINST PERPETUITIES § 629, at 599 (4th ed. 1942).

all," within 21 years of **any** life in being, the interest is valid, even if you cannot guarantee the interest satisfies the timeframe for other lives in being. Here's an illustration of the applicable timeline:

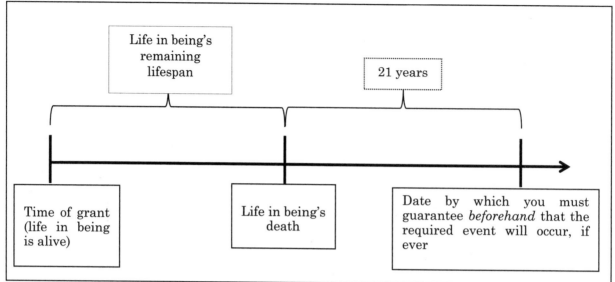

- This brings us to the final issue—what must happen within 21 years of a life in being? The interest must "vest, if at all." As will be explained more below, your task is to determine if the interest is guaranteed either to meet the definition of vesting or to cease to exist within 21 years of the death of a life in being, a person alive at the time of the grant or devise. In other words, an interest cannot continue in its "non-vested" state for more than 21 years after all lives in being—all people alive at the time of the grant or devise—have died.

> Ask whether the interest *must* vest, if at all, within the required time period. Even if it *might* vest or cease to exist within 21 years of a life in being, you must be able to *guarantee* that it will either vest or cease to exist within that time period.

That is a lot to digest; it is easier to see the RAP in operation than to memorize its component parts. We will now look at how to analyze these principles for the two types of remainders to which the RAP applies—contingent remainders and remainders to a class of people.

C. APPLYING THE RAP TO CONTINGENT REMAINDERS

For contingent remainders, "vest" means essentially what it says—a contingent remainder must not remain contingent beyond one generation after the remainder is created. "If at all" means that the remainder might not vest—it could, e.g., expire or be destroyed—but if the contingent remainder continues to exist, it must not remain contingent for more than 21 years after the death of everyone alive at the time of the grant. You must be able to guarantee that a contingent remainder will either go away (e.g., expire or be destroyed) or vest—thus, no longer be a contingent remainder—no later than 21 years after the death of someone alive when the contingent remainder is created. Stated another way, a remainder cannot remain contingent for longer than 21 years after all lives in being—everyone alive at the time of the grant or devise—have died. (You should reread this paragraph a few times after studying the examples that follow.)

Consider this example:

O to A for life, then to B and his heirs if B marries C (B has not married C)

Following the steps recommended in section B above, first analyze the state of the title on the face of the grant (meaning, what the language created). A owns a life estate, B owns a contingent remainder in fee (because of an as yet unmet condition precedent), and O has retained a reversion. Next, ask yourself if the grant creates any interest that the RAP can invalidate? Yes, the RAP can invalidate contingent remainders and thus B's interest must be tested to make sure it cannot possibly exist in its contingent state beyond one generation of those alive at the time the contingent remainder was created (i.e., 21 years after a life in being). Your task is not to save the remainder or to guarantee that it will vest, but rather to test whether it could stay contingent for too long—more than 21 years after all lives in being at the time of the grant. The lives in being that we know exist at the time of the grant are O, A, B, and C (these letters signify names and thus born persons). Is it possible that the remainder could exist indefinitely as a contingent remainder? No, it is only possible for B to marry C while both are alive (dead people do not marry). B's remainder will either vest during the lives of B and C, or it will never vest; regardless, it cannot continue as a contingent remainder indefinitely, specifically, not beyond the lives of B and C, and thus not beyond 21 years after both are dead. B and C are *validating lives* because they establish that the interest is valid under the RAP. A is an additional validating life because of the doctrine of destructibility. If B does not marry C by the expiration of A's life estate (by A's death), B's remainder will be destroyed for failure to vest on time. Thus, we know this contingent remainder cannot remain contingent indefinitely; it will either vest or it will go away at the death of A, B, or C.

Compare this example:

O to A and the heirs of his body, then to B and his heirs if B marries C (B has not married C)

A owns a fee tail, B owns a contingent remainder (condition precedent not yet fulfilled), and O has retained a reversion (following the contingent remainder). The RAP can invalidate a contingent remainder and thus B's interest must be tested. As above, B's contingent remainder is still valid. B must marry C during their lives or his remainder will never vest (it will go away when either B or C dies without them having married). B and C are therefore validating lives. However, unlike the previous example, A is not a validating life because the fee tail is not inherently limited to A's lifetime because it will continue beyond A's life if A dies with a bodily heir.

Now consider this example:

O to A for life, then if state-sponsored prayer returns to public schools, to B and his heirs

A owns a life estate, B owns a contingent remainder (condition precedent not yet fulfilled) in fee, and O has retained a reversion (following the contingent remainder). Again, we must apply the RAP to B's contingent remainder. Notice a red flag here—on its face, the condition precedent that makes the remainder contingent is potentially perpetual. State-sponsored prayer could return to public schools at any time (or never), and that condition is not tied to any particular person's lifetime or one generation beyond those currently alive (O, A, or B). In other words, on its face, this condition is potentially perpetual and not connected to any life in being. However, because of the destructibility rule, B's contingent remainder must vest by A's death or it will be destroyed for failure to vest in time. Solely because of destructibility, A is a validating life and the remainder is valid under the RAP. Remember, you do not have to guarantee that state-sponsored prayer will return to the public schools—you simply test whether, if it does return, it must do so within 21 years of a life in being. State-sponsored prayer may never return, but if it does not and remainders are destructible, the remainder will be destroyed at A's death, making A the validating life.

Compare this example:

> *O to A and the heirs of his body, then if state-sponsored prayer returns to public schools, to B and his heirs*

On the face of the grant, A owns a fee tail, B owns a contingent remainder in fee (condition precedent not yet fulfilled), and O has retained a reversion (following the contingent remainder). B's contingent remainder must be tested to see if it withstands the RAP. You do not have to guarantee that state-sponsored prayer will ever return; rather, if it does, you must know that it will do so within 21 years of the lifetime of some life in being. Our lives in being are O, A, and B. There is no validating life because this facially indefinite condition precedent could be met more than 21 years after all of the lives in being have died. B's contingent remainder is thus void under the RAP. What about destructibility? This remainder will be destroyed if it does not vest by the expiration of the preceding estate, but here, that estate is a fee tail, which could exist indefinitely beyond A's death. Therefore, unlike the previous example, A is not a validating life. What is the resulting state of the title after the RAP invalidates B's contingent remainder? Clearly, the remainder must be struck, but it would not make sense to strike only the remainder, which would leave a grant that would make no sense:

> *O to A and the heirs of his body, then if state-sponsored prayer returns to public schools*

You must therefore strike **both** the condition precedent **and** the remainder, leaving:

> *O to A and the heirs of his body*

The resulting state of the title is A owns a fee tail, and O has retained a reversion.

Savings Clause: The grantor can save a contingent remainder from the RAP by adding a clause tied directly to the lifetime of a life in being. For example, the contingent remainder in the conveyance immediately above could be saved if it were amended as follows:

> *O to A and the heirs of his body, then if state-sponsored prayer returns to public schools, to B and his heirs, <u>if B is then living</u>*

or like this:

> *O to A and the heirs of his body, then if state-sponsored prayer returns to public schools <u>during B's lifetime or within 21 years of B's death,</u> to B and his heirs*

Both of these savings clauses tie the condition precedent that makes B's remainder contingent to B's lifetime, making B the validating life and saving the contingent remainder from being void under the RAP.

D. APPLYING THE RAP TO CLASS REMAINDERS

The second interest the RAP applies to is *a remainder to a class of persons*, such as "the children of A", e.g., a *vested remainder subject to open*. In order to be valid under the RAP, a class remainder must close—thus, no longer be subject to open—within 21 years of a life in being. In other words, there cannot be any possibility that the remainder can still be open to more owners for longer than 21 years after all lives in being—everyone alive at the time of the grant or devise—have died. Two related common law rules apply when there is a remainder to a class:

> A class interest closes: 1) when the parent dies (9 months are added for a man), if the class is for the parent's children; or 2) as soon as the estate preceding the remainder expires.

- *A class identified solely as children of a person closes when that parent dies.* This is literally true if the gift is to the children of a woman, because she cannot have children after she dies (modern technology aside). However, if the person is a man, the period of gestation (9 months) is added, because his child could be born after his death. A child in the womb when the father dies is therefore eligible for membership in the class if the child is born within 9 months of the father's death.

Thus, for this conveyance:

O to A for life, then to the children of B

B is a validating life for the remainder because the class will close at B's death if B is a woman, or within 9 months of B's death if B is a man. This rule does not, however, save a remainder to a class that is identified by more than just being a child of a person, for example:

O to A for life, then to the children of B who attend State University

Here, we cannot guarantee the class will close at B's death, or 9 months later if B is a man, because the definition of ownership is not simply being a child of B. (Note, however, that A is a validating life due to the destructibility rule, and so this remainder is valid under the RAP.)

- *As soon as the estate preceding the class remainder expires, the class closes.* This is known as the *Rule of Convenience*.

Consider this example:

O to A for life, then to A's children who reach 30 and their heirs
(A has one child, X, age 31)

A owns a life estate, and X owns a vested remainder, subject to open, in fee. The class remainder must be tested by the RAP. It is possible that A might have another child who will reach 30 more than 21 years after O, A and X have all died. In other words, what if O and X die, A then has a second child, Y, and then A dies a year after Y is born? If Y reaches 30, it will be 29 years later—more than 21 years after all known lives in being (O, A, and X) have died. It appears on the face of things that none of our lives in being are guaranteed to be a validating life. Nevertheless, even though this class remainder could theoretically remain subject to open for more than 21 years after the last life in being, the Rule of Convenience provides that once the preceding estate (A's life estate) expires (at A's death), the class closes as a matter of law and the remainder becomes possessory. A is therefore the validating life because the class closes, at the latest, when A dies. The Rule of Convenience will cut off Y from sharing in ownership with X if Y does not turn 30 before A dies. As a consequence, the remainder is only subject to open *while it is a remainder*. In sum, the Rule of Convenience saves any vested remainder subject to open following a life estate owned by someone who is alive at the time of the grant and who is therefore a life in being.

Consider another example:

O to A for life, then to B's children (B has one child, X)

On the face of the conveyance, A owns a life estate, and X owns a vested remainder, subject to open, in fee. We must test whether the class interest is valid under the RAP. There are two validating lives that save X's remainder. First, because we assume normal biological reproduction, the class of B's children must close when B dies if B is a woman, or 9 months thereafter if B is a man. Either way, it is clear that the class cannot be subject to open for more than 21 years after the death of B, making B a validating life. Second, because the Rule of Convenience will close the class when A dies, the class cannot remain open beyond A's lifetime. A is therefore also a validating life. X's interest is valid under the RAP.

Contrast this example:

O to A in fee tail, then to B's children (B has two children, X and Y)

At the time of the grant, A owns a fee tail, and X and Y own a vested remainder, subject to open, in fee.[5] We must test the class interest to see if it is valid under the RAP. An owner of this remainder simply has to be a child of B. The class of B's children will be finally defined, and thus will close, at B's death if B is a woman, or 9 months after B's death if B is a man. Either way, it is clear at the time of the grant that the interest will not be subject to open for more than 21 years after the death of B. B is therefore a validating life, and the remainder is valid. This again assumes normal biological reproduction.[6]

Notice, however, that the Rule of Convenience does not provide an independent basis for saving the remainder. Because A owns a fee tail, if he has bodily heirs, his estate will pass to them, and so on, as long as his bloodline continues. The fee tail might not expire for more than 21 years beyond the death of the last life in being. Even though the class must close when the preceding estate, the fee tail, expires, we cannot be sure that the fee tail will expire soon enough to satisfy the RAP. Nonetheless, there only needs to be one validating life to save an interest under the RAP, and because B is a validating life, the interest stands.

Consider another example:

O to A for life, then to B's children who become astronauts
(B has one child, X, and X is an astronaut)

On the face of the grant, A owns a life estate and X owns a vested remainder, subject to open, in fee. Because this is a class remainder, it must be tested to see if it withstands the RAP. The Rule of Convenience saves X's interest. As soon as A dies, the class will close and the class remainder will become possessory. A is therefore a validating life, and the remainder is valid under the RAP. However, B is not a validating life. Although the class of "B's children" would close at B's death if B is a woman, or 9 months later if B is a man, the grant requires the owners to be astronauts, not just children of B. This class could remain open well beyond 21 years after B dies, because B's children could become astronauts more than 21 years after B dies. Neither is X a validating life, because another child of B could become an astronaut more than 21 years after X dies. However, you only need one validating life, and here A qualifies due to the Rule of Convenience, so the remainder is valid under the RAP.

One last example:

O to A in fee tail, then to B's children who reach age 30 (B has no children)

On the face of the grant, A owns a fee tail, B's children who reach age 30 own a contingent remainder (the owner is unascertained) in fee, and O has retained a reversion (following the contingent remainder). We must test the class remainder under the RAP. The lives in being are O, A, and B. Does the Rule of Convenience save the contingent remainder? It does not; although the class must close at the expiration of the preceding estate, a fee tail could continue indefinitely as long as A has living bodily heirs (issue). None of our lives in being (O, A, and B) are validating lives. Although B's children must be born during B's lifetime if B is a woman, or within 9 months of B's death if B is a man, the class is "B's children who reach age 30," not simply "B's children." We cannot be certain that all of B's children will turn 30 within 21 years of the death of O, A, or B. B might have one or more children who are born shortly before O, A, and B all die. If that would happen, B would have at least one child and thus a bodily heir, the fee tail would not expire at B's death, and some of B's children could reach age 30 more than 21

---

[5] As noted in Chapter 3, the law of concurrent estates, which will be covered later in your Property course, addresses the issue of how X and Y would own the fee together at the expiration of the fee tail.

[6] As you can see, modern reproductive technology will create obvious complexities for the law of estates and future interests in general and the RAP in particular. For simplicity, this book follows the common law presumption of normal biological reproduction and thus (artificially) puts modern reproductive technology aside, but this issue will certainly lead to litigation in the future.

years after all the lives in being have died. When we strike the invalid remainder, we are left with:

O to A in fee tail

After applying the RAP, A owns a fee tail, and O has retained a reversion.

CHAPTER 4 SUMMARY

The Rule in Shelley's Case: When the grantor conveys an interest in a life estate to a grantee, any remainder in that grantee's heirs in the same grant is treated as a remainder in the grantee.

The Rule against Perpetuities:

1) A contingent remainder is void if there is **any possibility** it will still be contingent more than 21 years after everyone alive when the remainder was created (particularly, everyone mentioned in the deed or will) has died.

2) A remainder to a class is void if there is **any possibility** it will still be subject to open more than 21 years after everyone alive when the remainder was created (particularly, everyone mentioned in the deed or will) has died.

If you can absolutely guarantee that:

a. A contingent remainder will either vest or no longer exist, or

b. A class remainder will either close or no longer exist

within 21 years of the lifetime/death of someone alive at the time of the grant (particularly, anyone mentioned in the deed or will), then you have a *validating life* and the interest is valid under the RAP.

E. PRACTICE PROBLEMS

Answer problems 1–7.

1. When does the Rule in Shelley's Case apply?

2. What is the result of applying the Rule in Shelley's Case?

3. Does the Rule Against Perpetuities apply to all future interests?

4. What is a life in being?

5. What is the time limitation of the RAP?

6. For an interest to be valid under the RAP, do we have to know that it will eventually vest within the applicable time limitation?

7. When do you apply the RAP?

For problems 8–11, give the state of title on the face of the grant. If the Rule in Shelley's Case applies, give the state of title afterwards.

8. O conveys Blackacre to A for life, then to A's heirs in fee.

9. O conveys Blackacre to A for life, then to B for life, then to B's heirs.

10. O conveys Blackacre to A for life, then to B for life, then to A's heirs.

11. O conveys Blackacre to A for life, then to all of A's children (A has no children).

For problems 12–23, first give the state of title on the face of the grant. Identify any interests that are threatened by the RAP. Test the interests, and give the state of title after applying the RAP. Apply the Rule in Shelley's Case and the Doctrine of Destructibility of Contingent Remainders as applicable.

12. O to A for life, then to B if humans walk on Mars.

13. O to A and the heirs of her body, then to B if B lives to be 75 (B is not yet 75).

14. O to A for life, then to A's children (A has one child, B).

15. O to A for life, then to the first person to walk on Mars.

16. O to A for life, then to B if B learns to play chess (B has never played chess).

17. O to A in fee tail, then to B if B becomes a CEO (B is not yet a CEO).

18. O to A for life, then to A's children who reach 21 (A does not yet have any children).

19. O to A for life, then to B if B's grandchildren graduate high school (none of B's grandchildren have yet graduated high school).

20. O to A in fee tail, then to B if Greece leaves the Eurozone.

21. O to A for life, then to A's youngest grandchild then living for life, then to O's oldest child then living for life, then, if any of A's other grandchildren are still alive, to those grandchildren.

22. T devises Blackacre to A, his child with a disability, for life, then for life to the last person who cares for A for more than 15 years, then to T's oldest descendant then living.

23. T executes a will devising Blackacre to A for life, then to B for life, then for life sequentially to each of A's children alive at T's death, beginning with the eldest, then for life to the next eldest until all A's children alive at T's death have owned Blackacre, then to the eldest then living descendant of A in fee. At the time, A has no children. Ten years later, T dies. He never sold Blackacre or changed his will, and A has two children, C and D (C is older than D).

Problems 24 and 25 explore two legal concepts that flow from the RAP. Remember, the RAP is concerned with what is theoretically possible, not with what is most probable. Give the state of title.

24. O conveys Blackacre to A in fee tail, then to A's last child to reach age 30 (A is 80 and she has two children, ages 50 and 40).

25. O conveys Blackacre to A for life, then to A's widow for life, then to A's children alive at A's widow's death.

F. CLASS DISCUSSION PROBLEMS

For problems 1–11, first give the state of title on the face of the grant. Identify any interests that are threatened by the RAP. Test the interests, and give the state of title after applying the RAP. Apply the Rule in Shelley's Case and the Doctrine of Destructibility of Contingent Remainders as applicable.

1. O to A for life, then to B's children who move to Texas (B has one child, X, who just moved to Texas).

2. O to A for life, then to B's children who move to Texas (B does not have any children).

3. O to A and the heirs of his body, then to O's children who visit the Alamo (O has one child, X, but X has never visited the Alamo).

4. O to A for life, then to B's children (B has no children).

5. O to A in fee tail, then to B if B masters backgammon (B does not know how to play backgammon).

6. O to A for life, then to B for life if B learns to play the piano, then for life to A's first child who learns to play the piano, then to A's heirs (A does not have any children, and B does not know how to play the piano).

7. O to A for life, then for life to O's children who join the military (O has one child, B, who has joined the military).

8. T devises Blackacre to A for life, then for life to T's last child to get married, then to A's heirs in fee tail.

9. O grants Blackacre to A for life, then to O's children alive at A's death for life, then to O's grandchildren.

10. T devises Blackacre to A for life, then to T's children alive at A's death for life, then to T's grandchildren.

11. O grants Blackacre to A and his bodily heirs, then to O's first child to turn 22 (O has two children, Z who is 19, and X who is 21).

For problem 12, read the fact pattern. Give the state of title after each event occurs.

12. Oscar conveyed Blackacre to his friend Albert for life, then—if Bryan (Oscar's son) learns to play guitar—to Bryan for life, then to Bryan's first child to learn to play the drums. At the time of the grant, Bryan had one child, Charlie. Neither Bryan nor Charlie played any instruments. Bryan, wanting to ensure that his son would eventually own Blackacre, paid for Charlie's lessons and Charlie became quite an accomplished drummer. On the other hand, Bryan lacked self-discipline and delayed taking guitar lessons.

After several years passed, Oscar grew homesick and attempted to reacquire everyone's interest in Blackacre so that he could again own it in fee. Only Albert and Charlie would sell their interests back; Bryan was quite unwilling to give up the chance of eventually owning Blackacre. Indeed, when Albert and Charlie sold their interests back to Oscar, Bryan finally determined to take guitar lessons. His first lesson was one week after Oscar bought Albert's and Charlie's interests back. Analyze the state of title on the face of the grant and after each event occurred.

Answer problem 13.

13. Suppose you are a practicing attorney, and a client asks you to edit his will. Your client, David, tells you Mapleacre has been the family farm for over 100 years. David thinks his son Chris would be inclined to sell Mapleacre as soon as David is gone. David wants Chris to be able to use Mapleacre when David dies, but he also wants his grandson, Micah, who loves farming, to have it someday. David wants to make sure Mapleacre stays in the family for as long as possible, even after Micah dies. How do you draft the will, without violating the RAP, to maximize the time someone in David's family will have an interest in Mapleacre? Do you need any additional information?

CHAPTER 5

DEFEASIBLE ESTATES FOLLOWED BY A FUTURE INTEREST IN THE GRANTOR

■ ■ ■

Until now, we have not examined present estates that can be cut short by the occurrence of some event. The fee lasts forever, and the life estate and the fee tail expire naturally—absent renunciation by the owner, none of these interests are cut off prematurely. Although a condition precedent might prevent a contingent remainder from ever vesting, it does not cut short an already possessory estate. In this chapter and the next, we will introduce estates that can be cut short—*defeasible* estates. "Defeasible" means the estate is subject to a condition that, if broken, can bring the estate to an end. We will consider four defeasible estates in this chapter, and two in the next chapter, as well as the future interests that follow these estates. Before we do so, however, it is very important to keep in mind that ***nothing we have learned thus far will change in this chapter***; we are adding to, not changing, the estates and interests learned. For example, it is still true, and always will be true, that a remainder only follows an expirable estate immediately at expiration.

A. DETERMINABLE ESTATES AND THE POSSIBILITY OF REVERTER

1. FEE SIMPLE DETERMINABLE

A fee simple determinable is a fee subject to a self-executing condition ("*determinable clause*") that, if broken, *automatically* (*as a matter of law*) ends the estate. The determinable clause is directly attached to the fee and is typically introduced by words of temporal limitation, most commonly, "as long as," "until," or "during":

> *O to A and his heirs as long as the property is used for farming purposes*
>
> *O to A until the land is farmed*
>
> *O to A as long as A does not divorce B*

> If a condition is attached to an estate (there is no punctuation between the condition and the estate) and is introduced by words of temporal limitation, the estate is determinable. Structurally, this is similar to a condition precedent directly attached to an interest, but a durational flag always makes the interest to which it is attached determinable, not contingent.

These determinable clauses are introduced by a temporal "flag" and are directly connected to the fee interest. In each instance above, A owns a *fee simple determinable*. If the condition is violated, the fee automatically ends by law.

2. LIFE ESTATE DETERMINABLE

The *life estate determinable* shares the same qualities as the fee simple determinable, except that the estate is for life and not in fee:

O to A for life as long as the property is used for farming purposes

O to A for life until the land is farmed

O to A for life as long as A does not divorce B

In each instance, A has a life estate determinable—a life estate that is subject to a condition which, if violated, automatically terminates A's interest as a matter of law.

3.   POSSIBILITY OF REVERTER

A *possibility of reverter* is the future interest O retains following a determinable estate and by which the grantee's title will automatically revert to O as a matter of law if the condition is violated. Let's return to the examples above:

O to A and his heirs as long as the property is used for farming purposes

O to A until the land is farmed

O to A as long as A does not divorce B

O to A for life as long as the property is used for farming purposes

O to A for life until the land is farmed

O to A for life as long as A does not divorce B

None of these conveyances expressly states what happens when and if the condition affecting A's fee simple determinable or a life estate determinable is violated. Because O started with full title, and only conveyed part of that title to A, O has implicitly retained the right to get title back if and when the condition is violated. The interest O has retained is a possibility of reverter. (Do not say "reverter" or "possibility of reversion"!)

> A possibility of reverter is the future interest O retains following a determinable estate, automatically giving O title if the condition is violated.

With a fee simple determinable (the first three examples above), A's fee reverts to O automatically, as a matter of law, if the stated condition is violated, leaving O with a fee simple.

With a life estate determinable (the last three conveyances above), A's life estate reverts to O if and when A violates the condition. This possibility of reverter is therefore for the life of A (a life estate pur autre vie). But notice that A's life estate is expirable, and O did not convey a remainder to another grantee. In these three conveyances, O therefore also retained a reversion, so full title will revert back to O when A dies, regardless of whether the condition is violated or not. O thus retained both a reversion (in fee, when A dies) and a possibility of reverter (for the life of A, in the event A violates the condition). If the condition on A's life estate is violated, O then would own a life estate pur autre vie (for the life of A) and a reversion. These two interests would merge, leaving O with a fee simple (life estate + reversion = fee).[1]

At common law, a possibility of reverter was inheritable, but not alienable or devisable. At modern law, a possibility of reverter is inheritable, alienable, and devisable.

---

[1]   You should see, and identify correctly, both interests that O retained. The common law considered the reversion to be a "greater" interest than the possibility of reverter and thus viewed the possibility of reverter as merging into the reversion, with the two interests combined labeled simply a reversion. That merger is reflected in the explanation above. However, to make sure that you identify and apply both interests correctly, this book will require you to label both interests separately.

B. ESTATES SUBJECT TO A CONDITION SUBSEQUENT AND THE RIGHT OF ENTRY

1. FEE SIMPLE SUBJECT TO A CONDITION SUBSEQUENT

A fee subject to a condition subsequent involves a condition that, if broken, gives the grantor the power to enter the property and terminate the fee; termination does not automatically happen as a matter of law. For this defeasible fee, the defeasance condition is introduced by conditional, rather than temporal, language (e.g., "but if" or "however"). Moreover, the condition typically follows and is set off from the present estate conveyed (and thus is a *condition subsequent*, because in the sequence of the grant the condition follows, or is subsequent to, the interest). For example:

> An estate is subject to a condition subsequent if the defeasance condition is introduced by conditional language and punctuation separates the defeasible estate from the conditional language.

O to A and his heirs, but if A ever stops using the property for farming purposes, then O may enter and reclaim the land

O to A, however, if A divorces B, then to O

In both grants, the defeasance clause is introduced by a conditional flag ("but if" or "however") and is not directly attached to the fee but instead introduces O's retained interest. Because this condition follows the fee, it is a condition subsequent. In both grants, A's fee is not automatically terminated if A violates the condition; O must enter and reclaim the land to terminate A's fee, and thus O can choose to overlook the violation and allow A to keep title. This is true for the second example, even though the grant does not explicitly say so. The language in the first example is technically more precise but both forms are acceptable.

> When distinguishing conditions precedent and subsequent, remember that a condition precedent can affect a remainder, making it contingent. Remainders always wait patiently; a condition subsequent introduces a future interest that can impatiently cut an estate short. A condition precedent either precedes or is directly attached to the interest it modifies. By contrast, a condition subsequent follows the estate the condition can cut short.

2. LIFE ESTATE SUBJECT TO A CONDITION SUBSEQUENT

This life estate in form mirrors the fee simple subject to a condition subsequent:

O to A for life, but if A ever stops using the property for farming purposes, then O may enter and reclaim the land

O to A for life, however, if A divorces B, then to O

3. RIGHT OF ENTRY

The *right of entry* is the interest O retains following an estate subject to a condition subsequent that allows O to enter and reclaim the estate.[2] To return to the examples above:

> The future interest O retains following an estate subject to a condition subsequent is a right of entry.

---

[2] This future interest is sometimes called a "power of termination," which reflects that O is empowered to terminate the grantee's estate at violation. The more common label "right of entry" will be used in this book.

O to A and his heirs, but if A ever stops using the property for farming purposes, then O may enter and reclaim the land

O to A, however, if A divorces B, then to O

O to A for life, but if A ever stops using the property for farming purposes, then O may enter and reclaim the land

O to A for life, however, if A divorces B, then to O

In each of these conveyances, O has retained is a right of entry, which is the right to enter and reclaim A's estate if the condition is violated. If, in the first two examples, O properly asserts the right of entry related to a fee subject to a condition subsequent, then O reclaims the fee. If A owns a life estate subject to a condition subsequent, as in the last two examples, O would enter and reclaim A's life estate. As with the life estate determinable, O has also retained a reversion following the expirable estate. If O enters and reclaims A's life estate, O will own a life estate pur autre vie (for the life of A) that will merge with O's reversion, leaving O with a fee. If O does not enter and reclaim A's life estate, O will still obtain the fee at A's death, via the reversion.

Like the possibility of reverter, at common law, a right of entry was inheritable but not alienable or devisable. At modern law, the right of entry is inheritable, alienable, or devisable.

To review, compare the following two conveyances:

O to A as long as the land is farmed

O to A and his heirs, but if the land is ever not farmed, then to O

The first conveyance creates a fee simple determinable. The condition (the land being farmed) is introduced by a temporal flag ("as long as") and is directly connected to A's estate (there is no punctuation between A's interest and the condition). If the land is ever not farmed, A's estate will automatically end. The conveyance does not identify who gets the property when A's estate ends, but because O retained whatever rights he did not give away, O retained a possibility of reverter. The second conveyance creates a fee subject to a condition subsequent. The condition uses conditional language, and it is separated by punctuation from A's estate. If the land is ever not farmed, then O may enter and reclaim A's fee. O retained a right of entry.

When a conveyance is ambiguous, the law disfavors automatic forfeiture and thus prefers an estate subject to a condition subsequent followed by a right of entry, rather than a determinable estate followed by a possibility of reverter. For example:

O to A as long as the land is farmed, then O can enter and reclaim

The two clauses are inconsistent; the present estate is a fee simple determinable, but the future interest is a right of entry. Here, the law would presume this ambiguous grant creates a fee subject to a condition subsequent and a right of entry.

To reinforce what you have learned, consider the following problem:

A client retains you and says he wants to give his land, Blackacre, to his cousin Louis, but, as a condition of ownership, he wants Louis to kick his habit of watching professional wrestling. What would you do? Think of all the questions you need your client to answer before you can prepare the deed of conveyance.

First, you need to ask your client to describe the type of interest he wants to convey to Louis—a "full title," i.e., one that will allow Louis to enjoy the property fully and also determine who owns it after his death (a fee simple), or a title that will allow Louis to enjoy the property while he is alive but not give him the right to determine who owns the property later (a life estate)? Let's assume that your client wants to convey "full title" and thus some sort of fee.

Does your client just want to restrict Louis's professional wrestling watching or also restrict later owners of the property (e.g., heirs/devisees) as well? Let's assume your client only wants to restrict Louis's use.

Does your client want to restrict Louis's watching of professional wrestling in general or just on the premises? Let's assume your client only wants to restrict Louis's activities on the premises.

Finally, does your client want the interest to terminate automatically if Louis violates the condition or does your client want to be empowered to take Louis's title away if he violates the condition? Let's assume automatically.

Based on the answers to the above questions, a fee simple determinable followed by a possibility of reverter would best serve your client's wishes. You should therefore draft the following conveyance:

Client to Louis and his heirs as long as Louis never watches professional wrestling on the premises

What if Louis dies without ever violating the condition? A fee simple determinable is devisable and inheritable, so the property goes to Louis's devisee if Louis has a will or to his heir if Louis dies intestate. What present estate will the devisee or heir then own? Although the grant created a fee simple determinable, the condition only restricted Louis's use of the property. If Louis never violated the condition, this estate is now functionally an unrestricted fee simple; Louis cannot watch professional wrestling on the premises after he dies. If your client wanted to restrict future users, the estate should have been subjected instead to the condition "as long as no one ever watches professional wrestling on the premises." In that event, Louis's devisee or heir would own a fee simple determinable at Louis's death.

Consider another problem, starting with the following conveyance:

O to First Baptist Church as long as the property is used for church purposes

The pastor of First Baptist Church, Jedd Clampitt, discovers oil on the property and then leases part of the land to an oil company. O, your client, seeks your advice regarding whether he now owns the property. How would you advise O? Do you need additional information?

The state of the title will depend on what the church is otherwise doing with the property. Read the conveyance carefully. If, in addition to the lease, the church continues to use the property for church purposes, then arguably the condition has not been violated, because the deed does not say the church must use the property "only" for church purposes. On the other hand, O could argue that "the property" means all of the property, and thus the condition is violated if the leased portion is not being used for church purposes. There are two lessons to learn here: avoid needless ambiguities when drafting conveyances, and always analyze the condition carefully to determine if it has in fact been violated.

C. STATUTES OF LIMITATION FOR POSSIBILITIES OF REVERTER AND RIGHTS OF ENTRY

Under modern law, there are two types of statutes that limit the existence of future interests O retains following a defeasible estate:

- Some jurisdictions limit how long a right of entry or a possibility of reverter can exist after being created, with 30 years being a typical time frame. After the time passes, the future interest is void and the estate is no longer defeasible. These statutes reflect the policy judgment that defeasance conditions lose utility over time and thus title should be cleared rather than encumbered indefinitely.

- Some jurisdictions also limit how long a holder of a right of entry can wait to enter and reclaim after the condition has been breached. If the right of entry is not exercised within that time (e.g., two years), the right is waived, the condition is void, and the estate is no longer defeasible.

CHAPTER 5 SUMMARY

Defeasible Estate: An estate that is subject to a condition that, if broken, can bring the estate to an end.

Determinable Estate: An estate subject to a self-executing condition that, if broken, automatically ends the estate. The condition is introduced by words of temporal limitation directly attached to the estate.

Possibility of Reverter: The future interest that the grantor retains following a determinable estate by which the grantor obtains the grantee's estate as a matter of law at violation of the condition attached to the grantee's estate.

Estate Subject to a Condition Subsequent: An estate subject to a condition that, if broken, gives the grantor the right to enter and reclaim the grantee's estate. The condition is introduced by a conditional flag, follows the estate grammatically, and is set off from the estate by punctuation.

Right of Entry: The interest the grantor retains following an estate subject to a condition subsequent by which the grantor has the right to enter and reclaim the grantee's estate at violation of the condition attached to the grantee's estate.

Statutes of limitation for possibilities of reverter and rights of entry:

- Some statutes limit how long a right of entry or a possibility of reverter can exist after being created (typically 30 years).
- Some statutes also limit how long an owner of a right of entry can wait to enter and reclaim after the condition has been breached; if the owner does not enter and reclaim, the defeasance clause is no longer enforceable.

D. PRACTICE PROBLEMS

For problems 1–5, identify the attributes of property ownership associated with each interest.

1. Fee simple determinable

2. Fee subject to a condition subsequent

3. Life estate determinable

4. Possibility of reverter

5. Right of entry

Answer problems 6–9.

6. Compare and contrast a determinable estate and an estate subject to a condition subsequent.

7. Compare and contrast a possibility of reverter and a right of entry.

8. What are the differences between a condition subsequent and a condition precedent?

9. What are the differences between a reversion and a possibility of reverter or a right of entry?

For problems 10–11, identify who owns the property once every event has occurred.

10. O conveys Blackacre to Caleb as long as chickens are raised on Blackacre. Caleb immediately starts raising chickens. When Caleb subsequently realizes that he could make more money by growing watermelons on the property, he butchers his chickens and plants melons.

11. O grants Blackacre to Christopher, but if Christopher stops taking piano lessons, then O retains the right to reenter and claim the property. At the time of the grant, Christopher is regularly taking piano lessons. After a few years—when he begins college—Christopher cancels his lessons. O never learns that Christopher has stopped taking lessons, and O never returns to Blackacre.

Provide the state of title for the conveyances in problems 12–21.

12. O to A for life as long as A regularly attends church.

13. O to A, but if A stops attending church, then O may reenter and claim the land.

14. O to A until a man walks on Mars.

15. O to A during the reign of Queen Elizabeth II.

16. O to A, but if Queen Elizabeth ceases to reign, then to O.

17. O to A for life, but if the Republicans gain a supermajority in both houses of Congress while a Republican is also president, then to O.

18. O to A and his heirs, but if A or one of his bodily heirs attends State University, then O may enter and reclaim the property.

19. O to A and his heirs as long as a natural gas well is operated on the property.

20. O to A for life while A farms the property.

21. O to A in fee tail, then to O's last child to graduate high school in fee tail, then to O's children who reach 20 and are employed by that age, otherwise to B and his heirs as long as the land is farmed (O does not yet have any children).

Problem 22 contains a pair of conveyances and a series of subsequent factual developments. For both grants, analyze the state of the title at the time of the grant and then at each point in the chronological chain. Assume there are no statutes of limitations.

22. O grants Greenacre to A as long as it is used for residential purposes.

O grants Greenacre to A, but if Greenacre is used for other than residential purposes, O may enter and reclaim.

a. A moves into the house on the day of the grant.

b. Four years later, A starts a computer repair business in his basement while continuing to live in the house.

c. One month after A opens his business, O tries to kick A out of the house.

Assume that your jurisdiction has a 30-year statute of limitations for possibilities of reverter and rights of entry. Moreover, assume that a right of entry must be exercised within two years of when the condition was violated. Give the state of title after each event in problems 23–24.

23. O conveys Blackacre to A in 2015. The conveyance states, "*O to A for life as long as A farms the property.*" Because of health problems, A stops farming in 2040. O attempts to enter and reclaim Blackacre in 2043.

24. O conveys Whiteacre to A in 2020: "*O to A, but if A ever uses Whiteacre for commercial purposes, then O may enter and reclaim the property.*" In 2030, A opens a garden nursery on Whiteacre; three years later, O claims title to the property.

E. CLASS DISCUSSION PROBLEMS

Provide the state of title for the conveyances in problems 1–10.

1. O to A, but if A opens a restaurant on the property, then to O.

2. O to A for life during A's service as Dean of State School of Law.

3. O to A, but if A does not marry B before A reaches age 30, then O may reenter and claim the land.

4. O to A for life until A obtains an MBA.

5. O to A, but if A becomes an attorney, then to O.

6. O to A for life as long as China has the world's largest population.

7. O to A for life, but if A does not visit O at least once each calendar year while O and A are both alive, then to O.

8. O to A, but if A does not open a bird sanctuary on the property, then to O.

9.   O to A as long as A visits O at least once a year while both are alive.

10.   O to A during A's career as an engineer.

Determine the state of title after each event in problem 11. If you do not have enough information to determine the state of title after every event, explain why.

11.   O conveys Blackacre to A for life, but if A starts smoking, O may enter and reclaim Blackacre. A does not smoke at the time of the grant, but A begins smoking sometime thereafter. When O learns of A's habit, O files suit to recover possession of and title to Blackacre.

Review and Integration: Provide the state of title for the conveyances in problems 12–22. Not all of these conveyances create defeasible estates; some interests are only followed by reversions or remainders as in previous chapters.

12.   O to A as long as A never drinks alcohol.

13.   O to A as long as no one uses illegal substances on the property.

14.   O to A for life, then to A's children then living.

15.   O to A, but if A opens a bar on the premises, then to O.

16.   O to A for life, then to B for life as long as B pays all taxes on the property.

17.   O to A for life, then to A's children as long as the property is used for residential purposes (At the time of the grant, A has one child, B).

18.   O to A for life, then to B for life, but if B opens a casino while he owns the property, then to O.

19. O to A for life, then to B if B survives A, otherwise to C, but if C does not reside on the property, then to O.

20. O to A for life, then to B for life if B becomes a chef, then to A's heirs (at the time of the grant, B is not a chef). Later, A conveys all title A has in the property to C, and B is still not a chef.

21. O to A in fee tail, then to B in fee tail if a human walks on Mars, then to C as long as NASA continues its space program.

22. O to A for life, then to A's son B for life if A continuously maintained a business on the property during A's lifetime, otherwise to C's children who reach 25 for life, then to D in fee tail if he or his wife ever owns a business, then to E. At the time of the grant, C has no children and D is one year old. Although A owns and operates a business on the property throughout his life, B dies before A. At B's death, C has twin sons, F and G, who are both 25. One year after B's death, D (who is now 27) gets married and starts a business. Seven years after D launches his business, A dies. Give the state of title at the time of the grant and after each event.

Problem 23 involves both legal and ethical considerations.

23. Your client O owns a large tract of land that he wants to subdivide, giving a portion to his only child and daughter, D. You agree to represent O to draft the deed and accept a retainer to do so. When you meet subsequently with O to obtain the necessary information to draft the deed, O indicates that he believes he only has a duty to provide for his daughter as long as she isn't married, and so O wants the property back if D ever marries. How would you advise O? How would you advise O if instead, for reasons O does not initially explain, O insists on conditioning the conveyance on D never marrying or entering into a civil union with another woman?

CHAPTER 6

DEFEASIBLE ESTATES FOLLOWED BY A FUTURE INTEREST IN A GRANTEE; EXECUTORY INTERESTS; THE DOCTRINE OF WORTHIER TITLE

■ ■ ■

In the last chapter, we learned the possibility of reverter and the right of entry, two future interests retained by the grantor that can cut off a prior estate. Under the English common law, before 1536, a grantor could not create an equivalent interest for a grantee; the only future interest the grantor could create for a grantee was a remainder. Because a remainder had to follow an expirable estate (life estate or fee tail) immediately, the grantor could not create a future interest that did anything else, e.g., cut off a defeasible fee or follow a gap after an expirable estate. This rule was often circumvented in courts of equity via the "use," which was similar to a modern trust, with the trustee carrying out the grantor's wishes to create interests that were not enforceable at law. Parliament subsequently adopted the Statute of Uses, which made interests created by use in equity enforceable at law, thereby expanding the interests that O could create at common law. This addition did not change remainders—they still only follow a life estate or fee tail immediately at expiration—but it created a new future interest, the *executory interest*. Once again, *we are adding to, not changing, what we've learned thus far*. We will now revisit the determinable estates, add another defeasible fee, and learn variants of the executory interest.

A. REVISITING DETERMINABLE ESTATES AND EXPANDING THE FUTURE INTERESTS THAT FOLLOW THEM

We previously learned a grantor implicitly retains a possibility of reverter when the grantor conveys only a fee simple determinable:

> *O to A as long as the property is used for residential purposes*

It is possible for the grantor instead to create and convey a future interest following a fee simple determinable:

> *O to A for as long as the property is used for residential premises, then to B*

In both instances above, A has a fee simple determinable; this is true in the second example even though O did not retain a possibility of reverter.

Similarly, the grantor can create and convey a future interest following a life estate determinable:

> *O to A for life as long as A farms the land, then to B*

A's interest is still a life estate determinable, even though O did not retain a possibility of reverter. We will see shortly how to classify B's interest in each of the above conveyances.

B. ESTATES SUBJECT TO AN EXECUTORY LIMITATION

Unlike a fee simple determinable, a fee subject to a condition subsequent cannot be followed by an interest in a grantee. Instead, where a defeasible fee is followed by an interest in a grantee, and a condition subsequent to the fee is introduced by a conditional flag and separated from the fee by punctuation, the estate is a *fee subject to an executory limitation*. For example:

O to A and his heirs, but if A ever marries C, then to B and his heirs

O to A, however, if the land is ever not farmed, then to B

These conveyances are structurally like a fee subject to a condition subsequent, but rather than O retaining the right to enter and reclaim, he instead conveys to a third party the right to take the property at violation. This defeasible fee is a fee subject to an executory limitation.[1] Unlike the fee subject to a condition subsequent, where O must enter and reclaim the property, this condition is self-executing, and therefore the fee is immediately cut off as a matter of law when the condition is violated.

> Structurally, the difference between an estate subject to a condition subsequent and one subject to an executory limitation is whether the grantor or a grantee owns the following future interest. An estate subject to an executory limitation automatically ends when the condition is violated; the fee subject to a condition subsequent does not.

It is also possible to have a life estate subject to an executory limitation:

O to A for life, but if A ever farms the land, then to B and his heirs

C. ANOTHER FUTURE INTEREST IN A GRANTEE— THE EXECUTORY INTEREST

In simple terms, an **executory interest** is a future interest conveyed to a grantee that is not a remainder. In other words, an executory interest does not wait patiently for an expirable estate to end naturally and then follow that estate immediately. It either cuts off a defeasible estate or follows an expirable estate but not immediately at its natural expiration. As you learned previously, whenever you analyze a conveyance where the grantor conveys a future interest to a grantee, you must first analyze whether it is a remainder. Does it wait patiently for an expirable estate (life estate or fee tail) to naturally expire? If it follows an expirable estate immediately at expiration, it is a remainder, and you then need to classify it completely (vested/contingent, present estate it will become, etc.). A remainder is still a remainder— everything you've learned thus far about remainders is true. If, however, the future interest conveyed to a grantee does something other than follow an expirable estate immediately at expiration, it is an executory interest. A remainder follows an expirable estate immediately; executory interests do everything else.

Let's reconsider the following examples from above:

O to A for as long as the property is used for residential premises, then to B

O to A for life as long as A farms the land, then to B

O to A and his heirs, but if A ever marries C, then to B and his heirs

O to A, however, if the land is ever not farmed, then to B

O to A for life, but if A ever farms the land, then to B and his heirs

In each conveyance, the future interest O conveyed to B is an executory interest. It is not a remainder because it does not follow an expirable estate immediately at expiration; instead, it cuts off A's estate (life estate or fee).

---

[1]   Some authorities call all determinable estates that are followed by a future interest in a grantee an "estate subject to an executory limitation." However, following the approach adopted by a majority of American jurisdictions, whenever a condition is directly attached to an estate by a temporal flag, we will call it a determinable estate regardless of whether the future interest is retained by the grantor (a possibility of reverter) or conveyed to a grantee (an executory interest).

Let's revisit two future interests that are not remainders that we first saw in Chapter 2:

O to A for life, then one year later to B and his heirs

O to A for life, then to B if B gives a proper burial for A

Because there is a gap between the life estate and the future interest, in both conveyances, B's interest is not a remainder but an executory interest.

D. TWO TYPES OF EXECUTORY INTERESTS

Now that you understand how to identify an executory interest, you next need to classify executory interests further. There are two types of executory interests—**shifting** and **springing**. The difference is easy to spot. On the face of the grant, see whether the executory interest cuts off an interest conveyed to a grantee (in which case it **shifts** from one grantee to another) or whether it follows and cuts off or ends an interest retained by the grantor (in which case it **springs** from the grantor to the grantee).

These conveyances that we considered above all create a shifting executory interest:

O to A for as long as the property is used for residential premises, then to B

O to A for life as long as A farms the land, then to B

O to A and his heirs, but if A ever marries C, then to B and his heirs

O to A, however, if the land is ever not farmed, then to B

O to A for life, but if A ever farms the land, then to B and his heirs

In each instance, B's interest follows and potentially cuts off an interest conveyed to A—title will shift from A to B at violation. In each instance, B has a shifting executory interest (in fee).

By contrast, these conveyances that we considered above both create a springing executory interest:

O to A for life, then one year later, to B and his heirs

O to A for life, then to B if B gives a proper burial for A

In both instances, A has a life estate, but B's future interest does not immediately follow A's life estate; there is a gap. The state of title, in the order in which the interests can become possessory, is A owns a life estate, O has retained a reversion (in fee subject to an executory limitation for one year or until the burial occurs, respectively),[2] and B owns an executory interest in fee. B's interest will spring from the grantor's interest—a reversion—rather than cutting off a grantee's interest. Do you see why O's reversion is not in fee simple absolute? After A dies, O gets the property in fee but subject to the limitation that, when the gap ends (in the first grant, once a year passes, and in the second, if B gives a proper burial for A), the property will spring to B. O has therefore retained a reversion in fee subject to an executory limitation followed by B's springing executory interest in fee.

Here is another springing executory interest:

O to A if and when A reaches 30 (A is not yet 30)

O has retained ownership of the present estate and has only conveyed a future interest to A. A's interest will cut off O's fee if and when A reaches 30. O has therefore retained a fee subject to an executory limitation (A reaching 30), and A has a springing executory interest in fee.

At common law, executory interests, like contingent remainders, were devisable and inheritable, but <u>not</u> alienable. Under modern law, executory interests are freely alienable and continue to be devisable and inheritable.

---

[2] This is an example of a reversion that is not in fee simple absolute, which was foreshadowed in Chapter 2.

E. COMPLEXITIES INVOLVING DEFEASIBLE LIFE ESTATES

Now that you understand executory interests, you can analyze defeasible life estates in more depth. Recall the following example of a life estate determinable:

O to A for life as long as A uses the property for farming purposes

As you learned in Chapter 5, O has implicitly retained both a possibility of reverter (A's life estate will revert to O if A violates the condition) and a reversion (in fee at A's death). Let's consider alternative scenarios regarding possible interests following A's life estate determinable.

First, rather than retain both future interests, O could retain one interest and convey the other to a grantee. For example, he could retain the possibility of reverter (for the life of A) and convey what would have been his reversion:

O to A for life as long as A uses the property for farming purposes, then at A's death to B

B's interest is a vested remainder in fee because it follows A's life estate at expiration, regardless of whether or not A violates the condition. If A stops farming the land and the property reverts to O, O will own a life estate pur autre vie (for the life of A), followed by B's vested remainder in fee.

O could instead retain the reversion and convey what would have been the possibility of reverter (for the life of A):

O to A for life as long as A uses the property for farming purposes, but if the land is not used for farming purposes, then to B for the life of A

In this case, B's interest is not a remainder because it will cut off A's life estate rather than patiently follow it. Thus, B has an executory interest, specifically a shifting executory interest for the life of A. If A stops farming the land, B will then own a life estate pur autre vie (for the life of A). O has retained a reversion and will take the fee at A's death whether or not A violates the condition.

Alternatively, O could decide to convey to B the right to take the property in fee at violation:

O to A for life as long as A uses the property for farming purposes, but if the land is not used for farming purposes, then to B

Because we presume B's interest is in fee, B has a shifting executory interest in fee. O has given B what was his possibility of reverter (for the life of A), plus he has carved out part of the reversion he retained. O will now own the property in fee at A's death only if A dies and never violated the condition. O still has a reversion (in fee), but it operates more narrowly than in the immediately preceding example.

Second, O could decide to convey both interests to B and could do so in a very cumbersome way:

O to A for life as long as A uses the property for farming purposes, but if A does not use the land for farming purposes, then to B, and regardless, at A's death, to B

This would give B both a shifting executory interest in fee and a vested remainder in fee. Fortunately, there is an easier way to effectuate O's intent:

O to A for life so long as A uses the property for farming purposes, then to B

Here, the law presumes that B will take the property both at violation of the condition (as a life estate pur autre vie for the life of A) and at A's death (in fee). In other words, it is presumed that O has conveyed both interests that he would have retained had he not created B's interest following A's interest. B has a vested remainder in fee that patiently follows A's life estate (this interest would have been O's reversion) and is certain to become possessory at A's death. B also has an executory interest for the rest of A's life estate, which becomes possessory if A ever stops farming the land (this interest would have been O's possibility of reverter had O retained it).[3] B will thus own the property in fee when the condition is violated (life estate pur autre vie + vested remainder in fee = fee) or, if A never violates the condition, at A's death (via the vested remainder in fee).

Finally, let's examine grants creating a life estate subject to an executory limitation. First, consider this conveyance:

O to A for life, but if A ever farms the land, then to B for the life of A

A has a life estate subject to an executory limitation, and B has a shifting executory interest for the life of A. Is that quantum? O has only expressly given B the right to take over A's life estate in the event A farms the land; O has not given B the right to take the property at A's death, nor has he explicitly conveyed a remainder following A's life estate. O therefore retained a reversion. If A dies without having farmed the land, O will own the property in fee (via the reversion), and B's executory interest will never become possessory. If A farms the land, B will then own a life estate for the life of A, and O will take the property in fee at A's death (via the reversion). Contrast this grant with the life estate determinable in the immediately preceding example above. In the life estate determinable example, B obtained both an executory interest <u>and</u> a remainder, whereas here, B obtains only an executory interest, while O retains a reversion.

Let's return to an example we considered earlier in this chapter:

O to A for life, but if A ever farms the land, then to B and his heirs

A has a life estate subject to an executory limitation, and B has a shifting executory interest in fee. At first glance, this may look like quantum, because the last interest is in fee, but look more closely. O has only expressly given B the right to take possession in the event A farms the land; O has not given B the right to take the property at A's death if A never farms the land, nor has he designated anyone to own a remainder following A's life estate. O therefore retained a reversion. If A dies without having farmed the land, B cannot take possession because the condition can now never be violated (A cannot farm the land after he dies). However, unlike the previous example where B's interest was in life estate pur autre vie (for the life of A), if A farms the land, here B will take the property in fee, not just for the life of A. O's reversion here therefore operates more narrowly than in the immediately preceding example above; O will take the property at A's death only if A never violates the condition and thus if B's interest never becomes possessory.

F. THE DOCTRINE OF WORTHIER TITLE

We previously learned one common law rule, the Rule in Shelley's Case, which clarified title by limiting O's ability to create certain future interests. Another rule that also was designed to clarify title is **The Doctrine of Worthier Title**, which provides that O cannot convey any future interest—either a remainder or an executory interest—to his own heirs. Any future interest that O grants to his own heirs is void and thus retained by O.

For example:

O to A for life, then to O's heirs

On its face, this would create a life estate for A and a contingent remainder for O's heirs (contingent because O's heirs cannot be ascertained until O dies). The Doctrine of Worthier

---

[3] Similar to how the common law would have viewed O's reversion as encompassing both a possibility of reverter and a reversion had O retained both interests, the common law here would view the remainder as the greater interest and thus would classify B's two interests simply as a vested remainder in fee. To make sure that you properly and fully identify B's property interests, this book will require you to list both future interests.

Title invalidates the remainder to O's heirs, thus leaving O with a reversion following A's life estate.

Unlike the Rule in Shelley's Case, which only applies to remainders, the Doctrine of Worthier Title applies to **any** future interest to O's heirs and thus **also** applies to executory interests. For example:

O to A, but if A uses the land for commercial purposes, then to O's heirs

On the face of this conveyance, A owns a fee subject to an executory limitation, and O's heirs own a shifting executory interest in fee. However, the Doctrine of Worthier Title invalidates the executory interest, essentially rewriting the conveyance to say:

O to A, but if A uses the land for commercial purposes, then to O

A therefore owns a fee subject to a condition subsequent, and O has retained a right of entry.

Likewise, consider this conveyance:

O to A as long as the land is used for residential purposes, then to O's heirs

On its face, this grant conveyed a fee simple determinable followed by a shifting executory interest in fee to O's heirs. The executory interest is invalid under the Doctrine of Worthier Title, leaving O with a possibility of reverter.

Today, most jurisdictions retain the Doctrine of Worthier Title but only as a presumption, not as a rule of law—that is, O can overcome the Doctrine if he makes the intent to do so clear. For example, O could explicitly state in the conveyance his awareness of the Doctrine and his intent that it not apply. Some jurisdictions have abolished the Doctrine and thus would effectuate O's intent and apply the grant as written.

CHAPTER 6 SUMMARY

A determinable estate may be followed by an interest in a grantee or in a grantor.

Estate Subject to an Executory Limitation: A defeasible estate that is followed by an executory interest in a grantee, and where a condition subsequent to the estate is introduced by a conditional flag and separated from the defeasible estate by punctuation.

Executory Interest: A future interest conveyed to a grantee that follows a defeasible estate.

Shifting Executory Interest: An executory interest that follows and cuts off an interest conveyed to a grantee in the original instrument (deed or will).

Springing Executory Interest: An executory interest that cuts off an interest retained by the grantor in the original instrument (deed or will).

The Doctrine of Worthier Title: This rule treats any future interest the grantor conveyed to the grantor's heirs as if the grantor retained the interest.

G. PRACTICE PROBLEMS

Answer problems 1–8.

1. A conveyance creates a defeasible fee; the condition is introduced by words of temporal limitation, and the condition is directly attached to the estate. The future interest is in the grantor. What is the present estate, and what is the future interest following it?

2. A conveyance creates a defeasible fee; the condition is introduced by conditional language, and punctuation separates the defeasible estate from the conditional language. The future interest is in the grantor. What is the present estate, and what is the future interest following it?

3. A conveyance creates a defeasible fee; the condition is introduced by words of temporal limitation, and the condition is directly attached to the estate. The future interest is in a grantee. What is the present estate, and what is the future interest following it?

4. A conveyance creates a defeasible fee; the condition is introduced by conditional language, and punctuation separates the defeasible estate from the conditional language. The future interest is in a grantee. What is the present estate, and what is the future interest following it?

5. What are the differences between a fee subject to a condition subsequent and a fee subject to an executory limitation?

6. What is the difference between a shifting and a springing executory interest?

7. To what interests does the Doctrine of Worthier Title apply?

8. How do you distinguish the Doctrine of Worthier Title from the Rule in Shelley's Case?

For problems 9–13, identify whether the executory interest is shifting or springing.

9. O grants Blackacre to A as long as A never fails to submit his federal tax return, then to B.

10. O grants Blackacre to A when A balances his budget.

11. O grants Blackacre to A, but if A incurs more than $5,000 in debt, then to B.

12. O grants Blackacre to A for life, then to B six months after A's death.

13. T devises Blackacre to A when A becomes a grandfather.

For problems 14–17, identify the defeasible fee that A owns as well as the future interest following it.

14. O grants Blackacre to A as long as the property is farmed, then to B.

15. O grants Blackacre to A, but if A ever joins the Navy, then O may enter and reclaim.

16. O grants Blackacre to A until A becomes a Marine.

17. T devises Blackacre to A, but if A runs for political office, then to B.

For problems 18–20, identify the defeasible life estate that A owns as well as the future interest(s) following it.

18. T devises Blackacre to A for life, but if A opens a bar on Blackacre, then to B.

19. O grants Blackacre to A for life as long as A remains a Libertarian, then to B.

20. O grants Blackacre to A for life, but if B quits smoking, then to B.

Provide the state of title on the face of the grant for problems 21–31. If the Doctrine of Worthier Title or the Rule in Shelley's Case applies, also provide the state of title after applying the rule(s).

21. O to A for life, then to O's heirs.

22. O to A, but if A ever starts smoking, then to O's heirs.

23. O to A as long as the land is farmed, then to A's heirs.

24. O to A for life, then to O's children (O has no children).

25. O to A for life, then to B for life, then to A's heirs.

26. O to A as long as the land is farmed, then to O's heirs.

27. O to A for life until A starts raising chickens, then at A's death to B.

28. O to A for life, but if A is ever elected to political office, then to B for the life of A.

29. O to A until A no longer makes maple syrup on the property.

30. O to A when A's first child is born (A has no children).

31. O to A, but if A stops farming the property or B graduates law school, then to B.

H. CLASS DISCUSSION PROBLEMS

For problems 1–6, identify whether and why the future interest Bob owns is a remainder or an executory interest, and then classify Bob's remainder or executory interest fully.

1. O to Alice for life, then to Jimmy for life, then, if Bob has married Sally, to Bob and his heirs as long as Bob does not use the property as a pig farm.

2. O to Alice and her bodily heirs, then one year later to Bob and the heirs of his body.

3. O to Alice and her heirs, but if Timmy attends Harvard University, then to Bob for life, remainder to Sally and her heirs.

4. O to Alice for life, then to Jimmy for life, but if Bob marries Sally, to Bob and his heirs as long as Bob does not use the property as a pig farm.[4]

5. O to Alice for life, then to Bob for life provided Bob has married Sally, otherwise to Jimmy and the heirs of his body.

6. O to Alice for life, then to Jimmy and his heirs as long as the property is not used for a pig farm, then to Bob and his heirs.

Putting it together: for problems 7–14, give the state of title.

7. O grants Blackacre to A when A reaches 50.

8. O grants Blackacre to A, but if A ever pastures poultry on the land, then to B.

9. O grants Blackacre to A for life, then six years later to B.

10. O grants Blackacre to A until B marries C, then to B.

11. O grants Blackacre to A for life as long as A regularly attends church.

12. O grants Blackacre to A for life as long as A practices optometry, but if A ever stops practicing optometry, then to B.

13. O grants Blackacre to A when O's last currently living child dies.

---

[4] Class Discussion Problem 15 in Chapter 7 will require you to assess the complete state of the title for this problem, including how to classify Jimmy's interest fully.

14. O grants Blackacre to A for life, then to B for life, but if B farms the land, then to O's heirs.

Problem 15 contains a pair of conveyances and two alternate factual developments. For both grants, analyze the state of the title at the time of the grant and then for each alternate factual situation.

15. O grants Blackacre to A as long as A survives B, then to B (both A and B are alive).

O grants Blackacre to A, but if A predeceases B, then to B (both A and B are alive).

a. B dies five years later, and A is still alive.

b. A and B are killed simultaneously in a car accident ten years later.

CHAPTER 7

THE EFFECT OF EXECUTORY LIMITATIONS ON VESTED REMAINDERS

■ ■ ■

You have previously learned how executory limitations can cut short a present possessory estate. For example:

O to A, but if B graduates college before A, then to B

This executory limitation can cut short A's fee simple subject to an executory limitation. A's interest is a present estate, and the executory limitation introducing B's shifting executory interest affects what happens afterwards.

Executory limitations can also affect remainders:

O to A for life, then to B, but if C graduates college before B, then to C

Because the vested remainder is a future interest—not a present estate—the executory interest might affect the remainder before it ever becomes a present estate, or, in this case, perhaps after it becomes a present estate. We need to learn how to classify such interests fully, but before we do so, it is first important to clarify how to distinguish contingent from vested remainders where the remainder is followed by an executory interest.

A. DISTINGUISHING CONDITIONS PRECEDENT, CONDITIONS SUBSEQUENT, AND DETERMINABLE CLAUSES

First, let's review the different types of conditions we have learned thus far.

A *condition precedent* is introduced by a conditional flag (typically "if") and either precedes an interest or is directly attached to it. The following grants contain a condition precedent to B's remainder:

O to A for life, then if B marries C, to B

O to A for life, then to B if B marries C

In both cases, the condition must be met for the remainder to become possessory, and thus the condition is a condition precedent and makes the remainder contingent, assuming B has not yet married C.

A *condition subsequent* follows, and is set off by punctuation from, an interest, and is introduced by a contradictory conditional flag (e.g., "but if" or "however"):

O to A for life, then to B, but if B divorces C, then to O

The remainder is not contingent, because the condition neither precedes nor is directly attached to B's remainder. Rather, the condition is subsequent to B's remainder and introduces a right of entry, leaving B with a vested remainder in fee subject to a condition subsequent.

A *determinable clause* involves a condition that is introduced by a temporal flag ("as long as," "until," "during") and directly attached to the interest:

O to A for life, then to B as long as B does not farm the land

This condition only affects the remainder after it becomes possessory. It is a determinable clause, rather than a condition subsequent or precedent, leaving B with a vested remainder in fee simple determinable.

The differences between these three types of conditions are essential to analyze how executory interests affect, and interrelate with, remainders.

B. DISTINGUISHING CONTINGENT AND VESTED REMAINDERS FOLLOWED BY AN EXECUTORY INTEREST

As we learned previously, a remainder is contingent when the owner is unascertained or the remainder is subject to an unfulfilled condition precedent. What if a remainder is followed by an executory interest that can cut off the remainder? Is the remainder vested or contingent? As usual, it is best to see examples as you learn the applicable rules.

You must first determine that you have a remainder, a future interest that immediately follows an expirable interest (life estate or fee tail). Again, everything you have learned about identifying remainders is still true, and by now you should be able to distinguish remainders from executory interests.

Next, you must determine whether the condition is introduced by a temporal or conditional flag. *A temporal flag <u>always</u> makes the interest determinable, rather than conditional/contingent.* For example:

O to A for life, then to B and his heirs as long as the land is farmed

The "as long as" flag is temporal and thus affects B's interest *only after* B takes possession. B's remainder is therefore not contingent; B owns a vested remainder in fee simple determinable. B will get possession of Blackacre when A dies, and when B takes possession, he will own a fee simple determinable, followed by the possibility of reverter O implicitly retained.

Once you have determined that the conditional language in a grant is not a determinable clause, you must then ascertain if the language creates a condition precedent or a condition subsequent. A condition precedent either precedes the remainder or is grammatically attached to it, while a condition subsequent follows and is set off from the remainder. To make this assessment, *stop at each punctuation point and classify the interest to that point*.

Compare the following conveyances:

> Executory limitations can affect vested remainders. To evaluate the state of title, determine if a remainder exists and if it is vested. ***Stop at each punctuation point, identify the interest to that point, and classify the interest.***

O to A for life, then if B has married C, to B

O to A for life, then to B if B has married C

O to A for life, then to B, but if B has not married C by A's death, then to D

In each conveyance, B's interest is clearly a remainder, because it directly follows A's life interest, an expirable estate. B's remainder is not determinable—there is no temporal flag introducing a determinable clause—but rather is conditioned on whether B marries C. In the first grant, the marriage condition is a condition precedent because it immediately precedes B's interest and is introduced by the conditional flag "if." In the second grant, the marriage condition is a condition precedent because it is grammatically attached to B's interest by the conditional flag "if." By contrast, in the third conveyance, the marriage condition *follows* B's interest, is set off by a comma, and is introduced by the contrary conditional flag "but if." The condition on B's remainder in the third conveyance is a condition *subsequent*, not a condition precedent.

You may ask how the condition in the third example can be "subsequent" to B's remainder when, by its express terms, it will affect B's remainder only up to A's death and thus before B takes possession? Excellent question! ***Conditions subsequent and precedent are distinguished <u>solely</u> by the sequential placement of the condition in the grant, including the placement of punctuation.*** In other words, ***they are precedent or*** *subsequent in terms of <u>grammatical sequence</u> in the grant, <u>not</u> in terms of chronological events*. "Condition subsequent" therefore means *subsequent in the sequence of the wording of the grant, not subsequent in terms of when the event could occur*. The condition "but if B has not married C by A's death" is subsequent to B's remainder because it follows, and is set off from, B's remainder in the wording of the grant. The timing of when the condition could affect the remainder has nothing to do with whether the condition is classified as precedent or subsequent (but as we shall see below, this timing *does* affect ways to classify remainders further).

Remember, a *condition makes a remainder contingent <u>only</u> if it is a condition <u>precedent</u>*. This is why B's remainder in the third example is vested, not contingent. The "stop at each punctuation point" rule verifies this conclusion. In each of these conveyances, respectively, if you stop at the comma after B's remainder, you have this:

> *O to A for life, then if B has married C, to B*
>
> *O to A for life, then to B if B has married C*
>
> *O to A for life, then to B, . . .*

You should clearly see that the first two remainders are contingent, but now you should also see more clearly why B's remainder in the third grant is vested: B is born and ascertainable, and there is no condition precedent that affects B's remainder. And yet, as we know from the full conveyance,

> *O to A for life, then to B, but if B has not married C by A's death, then to D*

a condition subsequent can affect B's vested remainder. We now need to classify B's vested remainder more fully based on how the condition subsequent can affect it.

C. THREE VESTED REMAINDERS FOLLOWED BY AN EXECUTORY INTEREST

When a condition subsequent follows a vested remainder and introduces an executory interest, there are three possible ways to classify the vested remainder. To distinguish the three possibilities, you need to consider whether the executory limitation and interest can affect the remainder only while it is a remainder, only after it becomes a present estate (and thus is no longer a remainder), or possibly either before *or* after it becomes a present estate.

1. VESTED REMAINDER, SUBJECT TO DIVESTMENT[1]

A vested remainder is subject to divestment when an executory interest *could* cut off the remainder *<u>only before</u> the remainder becomes a present estate* (thus, *only while it is still a remainder*). For example:

> *O to A for life, then to B, but if A ever opens a restaurant on the premises, then to C*

A owns a life estate. B owns a remainder because B's interest immediately follows A's life estate. C's interest is not a remainder because it does not wait patiently to follow an expirable interest immediately at expiration; C's interest will instead cut off B's remainder. C therefore owns a shifting executory interest in fee. We now need to classify B's remainder more fully. B's remainder is vested because B is the ascertained owner and there is no condition precedent to B's interest. How will the condition subsequent affect B's remainder? A must be alive to open a restaurant, which could only happen while A's life estate is still possessory and thus while B's interest is still a remainder. This executory limitation can therefore affect, and thus possibly

---

[1] As you learned in Chapter 3, a vested remainder subject to open is sometimes called a vested remainder "subject to partial divestment." This is a tangentially related but different concept. One reason we prefer the label "subject to open" for a remainder to a class is to avoid unnecessary confusion between these concepts.

cut off, B's remainder <u>only</u> while it is still a remainder, and thereby can only keep it from becoming a present estate. The executory interest can therefore only "divest" B's vested remainder. B owns a ***vested remainder, subject to divestment, in fee*** (***<u>not</u>*** a "vested remainder in fee subject to divestment"—the remainder, not the fee, is subject to divestment). If A violates the condition, at that time B's remainder would be divested and replaced by C's interest, which would become possessory in fee at A's death. If A dies not having violated the condition, C's executory interest will never become possessory, and B will own the property in fee.

Here is another example:

O to A for life, then to B, but if B marries A, then to C

For the same reasons as in the preceding example, A owns a life estate, B owns a vested remainder, and C owns a shifting executory interest in fee. How does this condition subsequent affect B's remainder? B cannot marry A after A dies (or to state it the other way, B can only marry A while A is still alive), so the executory interest can only affect B's remainder while A's life estate is still in existence and thus while B's remainder is still a remainder (before it becomes a present estate). B thus owns a vested remainder, subject to divestment, in fee. Graphically, the state of the title looks like this:

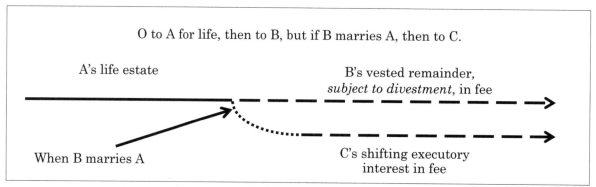

In the previous two examples, the conditions are subsequent to B's remainder because they are subsequent in the wording of the grant—they follow B's remainder, are set off by punctuation, and are introduced by "but if." In both cases, B's remainder is not contingent—there is no condition precedent—and thus is vested. However, because the remainder can be cut off before it becomes possessory, it is subject to divestment. Both of these examples look a lot like contingent remainders in that they involve remainders that will never become possessory if the condition is violated or not met. But they are vested, not contingent, solely because these are conditions subsequent, not conditions precedent. This may seem like a hairsplitting distinction, but it has important potential ramifications; e.g., only contingent remainders are destructible. Vested remainders, subject to divestment, are not destructible because they are vested, not contingent. (Yes, that is somewhat circular and arbitrary, but true nonetheless.)

2.   VESTED REMAINDER IN AN ESTATE SUBJECT TO AN EXECUTORY LIMITATION

A vested remainder is in an estate subject to an executory limitation when an executory interest ***could*** cut off the remainder ***<u>only after</u> the remainder becomes a present estate*** (thus, when it is no longer a remainder). For example:

***O to A for life, then to B, but if B ever opens a restaurant
on the premises, then to C***

Again, A owns a life estate, B owns a vested remainder, and C owns a shifting executory interest in fee. How does this condition subsequent affect B's remainder? Conditions regarding the owner's use of the property are presumed to apply only when the interest is possessory (for example, here, it would not matter if A let B open a restaurant on the property). This condition subsequent therefore cannot be violated until B's remainder becomes a present estate. In other words, the executory limitation cannot cut off B's interest while it is still a remainder but will only apply to B's interest after it becomes a present estate, making it defeasible. B owns a ***vested remainder in fee subject to an executory limitation*** (***not*** a "vested remainder subject to an executory limitation in fee"—the fee, not the remainder, is subject to the executory limitation).

Here is another example of a vested remainder in fee subject to an executory limitation:

> ***O to A for life, then to B, but if B does not re-landscape the property within one*** ***year of having the right of possession, then to C***

By its express terms, this condition will not affect B's remainder until after it becomes possessory. Graphically:

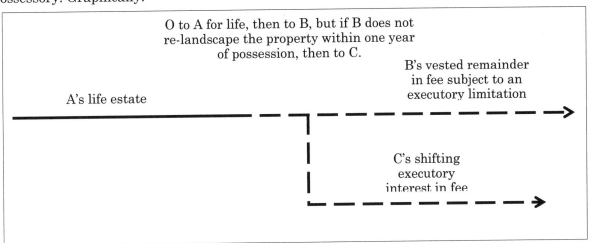

3. VESTED REMAINDER, SUBJECT TO DIVESTMENT, IN AN ESTATE SUBJECT TO AN EXECUTORY LIMITATION

A vested remainder is ***both*** subject to divestment ***and*** in an estate subject to an executory limitation when the executory interest ***could*** cut off the remainder ***either while the*** ***remainder is still a remainder or after it becomes a present estate***. For example:

> ***O to A for life, then to B, but if either A or B ever opens a restaurant on the*** ***premises, then to C***

If A opens a restaurant, then the executory limitation will divest B's remainder while it is still a remainder and thus keep it from becoming possessory. If A does not open a restaurant on the premises but B does, then the executory interest will cut off B's interest only after it becomes a present estate. Because this executory interest could affect B's remainder either before or after it becomes a present estate, B owns a ***vested remainder, subject to divestment, in fee*** ***subject to an executory limitation***. The same result would obtain if the condition subsequent involved generic use language not tied to a specific owner. For example:

> ***O to A for life, then to B, but if a restaurant is opened on the premises within*** ***20 years of the date of this grant, then to C***

This condition could be violated either before or after B's remainder becomes possessory (before or after A dies). B owns a vested remainder, subject to divestment, in fee subject to an executory limitation.

The same result can occur when the condition subsequent has nothing to do with the use of the property or who owns it:

> *O to A for life, then to B, but if C graduates college, then to C*

Because C could graduate college either before or after A's death, and thus either before or after B's remainder becomes possessory, the condition could affect B's interest as either a remainder or a present estate. B therefore owns a vested remainder, subject to divestment, in fee subject to an executory limitation.

D. A BRIEF FURTHER CLARIFICATION OF DEFEASIBLE LIFE ESTATES

Consider the following example:

> *O to A for life, then to B and his heirs, but if B attends Western State University, then to C and his heirs*

If B attends WSU, B's remainder will clearly be immediately cut off. But if A is still alive when B attends WSU, is A's life estate cut off too? In other words, does A own a life estate or a defeasible life estate; i.e., does the condition apply to the remainder only or also to the life estate?

Unless the grant makes it clear otherwise, a condition subsequent is presumed to be subsequent to, and thus to affect, **only** the interest to which it is **immediately** subsequent, not all interests that precede it. The grant must clearly establish the intent for the condition also to make the life estate defeasible; otherwise, the condition will only be construed to affect the interest to which it is immediately subsequent, here, B's remainder. A therefore has a life estate, not a life estate subject to an executory limitation. Can you see how to classify B's interest fully? B could attend WSU either before or after A dies. Because the condition could therefore affect B's remainder either before or after it becomes possessory, B has a vested remainder, subject to divestment, in fee subject to an executory limitation. C has a shifting executory interest in fee.

Consider another example:

> *O to A for life, then to B and his heirs, but if A ever farms the land, then to C and his heirs*

Even though this condition relates to A's use of the property, the grant still does not make it clear that the condition affects A's interest. The condition is subsequent only to B's vested remainder, not to A's life estate; A's farming the land will cut off only B's remainder, not A's life estate. A has a life estate, B has a vested remainder, subject to divestment, in fee, and C has a shifting executory interest in fee.

Contrast this conveyance:

> *O to A for life, then to B and his heirs, but if A ever farms the land, then <u>at that time</u> to C and his heirs*

Here, the grant makes it clear that C is to take the property at the moment A farms it ("at that time"). Thus, C's executory interest can cut off both A's life estate and B's remainder. A owns a life estate subject to an executory limitation, B has a vested remainder, subject to divestment, in fee, and C has a shifting executory interest in fee.

CHAPTER 7 SUMMARY

Distinguishing a Condition Precedent from a Condition Subsequent: A condition precedent either literally precedes the remainder or is directly attached to it, whereas a condition subsequent follows and is set off from the remainder.

An unmet condition precedent makes a remainder contingent; a remainder can be vested even if it is followed by a condition subsequent that introduces an executory interest.

Vested Remainder, Subject to Divestment: This exists when the executory limitation could cut off the remainder only *before* it becomes a present estate.

Vested Remainder in an Estate Subject to an Executory Limitation: This exists when the executory limitation could cut off the remainder only *after* it becomes a present estate.

Vested Remainder, Subject to Divestment, and in an Estate Subject to an Executory Limitation: This exists when the executory limitation could cut off the remainder while it is still a remainder or after it becomes a present estate.

A condition subsequent is presumed to affect only the interest that immediately precedes it unless the grant makes it clear that it affects other interests.

E. PRACTICE PROBLEMS

Answer problems 1–4.

1. When a remainder is subject to a condition, how can you determine whether the remainder is contingent or vested?

2. When is a vested remainder in an estate subject to an executory limitation?

3. When is a vested remainder subject to divestment?

4. When is a vested remainder both subject to divestment and in an estate subject to an executory limitation?

For problems 5–11, identify whether the vested remainder to B is subject to divestment, in an estate subject to an executory limitation, or both.

5. T devises Blackacre to A for life, then to B, but if B failed to visit T before his death, then to C.

6. O grants Blackacre to A for life, then to B, but if B ever stops providing for A's family after A's death, then to C.

7. O grants Blackacre to A for life, then to B, but if C publishes a book on Estates in Land and Future Interests, then to C.

8. O grants Blackacre to A for life, then to B, but if B digs a new well on the premises, then to C.

9. O grants Blackacre to A for life, then to B, but if A or B renovates the house on Blackacre, then to C.

10. T devises Blackacre to A for life, then to B, but if T's youngest child retires after A's death, then to that child.

11. O grants Blackacre to A for life, then to B, but if A ever leaves the law firm O founded, then to C.

For problems 12–17, determine whether B's interest is a contingent remainder or a vested remainder subject to divestment and/or in an estate subject to an executory limitation.

12. O grants Blackacre to A for life, then to B if B has learned to play the guitar.

13. O grants Blackacre to A for life, then to B, but if B has not yet learned to play the guitar, then to C.

14. O grants Blackacre to A for life, then to A's children (A has one child, B).

15. O grants Blackacre to A for life, then to A's son B, but if A has more children before his death, then to all of A's children (A has one child, B).

16. O grants Blackacre to A for life, then to O's only son B, but if O has more children, then to all of O's children.

17. O grants Blackacre to A for life, then if A does not have any sons, to O's son B (A has no children).

For problems 18–21, identify every interest that is subject to divestment and/or in an estate subject to an executory limitation.

18. O grants Blackacre to A for life, then to B, but if B ever leaves the law firm O founded, then at that time to C.

19. O grants Blackacre to A for life, then to B, but if B ever raises chickens on Blackacre, then to C.

20. O grants Blackacre to A for life, then to B, but if A voluntarily retires, then at that time to A's son C.

21. T devises Blackacre to A for life, then to B, but if T dies childless, then to T's brother C.

Putting it together: for problems 22 and 23, give the state of title.

22. O conveys Blackacre to A for life, then to B for life, but if C outlives A, then to C.

23. O conveys Blackacre to A for life, then to B for life unless B becomes a pilot, then to C, but if C becomes a pilot, then to D.

F. CLASS DISCUSSION PROBLEMS

For problems 1–4, assume the conveyance begins with this language: "I Thurston Howell III convey Goldacre to Lovey for life, then to...".   Classify each of the following future interests.

1. "Gilligan and his heirs, but if Gilligan attends Yale, then to the Professor and his heirs."

2. "Gilligan for life if Gilligan does not attend Yale, otherwise to the Professor and his heirs."

3. "Gilligan and his heirs, but if Gilligan holds a reception for Yale graduates on Goldacre, then to the Professor and his heirs."

4. "Gilligan and his heirs, but if Lovey donates money to Yale, then to the Professor and his heirs."

Putting it together: for problems 5–15, give the state of title.

5. O grants Blackacre to A for life, then to B if B has children at that time, otherwise to C for life.

6. O grants Blackacre to A for life, then to A's children, but if at that time any of A's living children are older than 50, then to C (A has one child, B, and B is 30 years old).

7. O grants Blackacre to A for life, then to B for life, but if C passes his law school Property course, then to C for life until C fails a class in law school.

8. O conveys Blackacre to A for life, then to B if B has children, otherwise to C.

9. O conveys Blackacre to A for life, then to B for life, then to C, but if A uses the property for commercial purposes, then at that time to D.

10. O conveys Blackacre to A for life, then to B for life as long as B has children in school, then to C.

11. O grants Blackacre to A for life, then to B for life, then to C, but if B sells illegal substances on the property, then to D in fee tail, then to E if E is not a drug dealer.

12. O conveys Blackacre to A for life, then to B for life, but if at any time B divorces his wife W, then at that time to C.

13. O conveys Blackacre to A in fee, but if A goes to law school, then to B for life, then to C for life, then to D, but if B, C, or D becomes an attorney, then to E.

14. O conveys Blackacre to A for life, then to B for life, then to A's children who reach 50, but if the land is used for farming within O's lifetime, then at that time to C (A has no children).

15. (Repeat of Class Discussion Problem 4 from Chapter 6) O to Alice for life, then to Jimmy for life, but if Bob marries Sally, to Bob and his heirs as long as Bob does not use the property as a pig farm.

For problem 16, assume you are a practicing attorney, and that a client desires your help drafting her will.

16. Anna, a family friend and long-time client, visits your office. After explaining that she is growing old and has been pondering her will, she tells you the following:

> I'm quite close with my niece, Barbara, who lives nearby, but she's been out of work because her employer went out of business, and she's having difficulty paying her rent. I invited her to live with me on my farm on Meadowacre, and after I die, I want her to own it for the rest of her life. Barbara isn't very young herself, and after her, I want one of my two children to own the farm. Debbie, the responsible one, moved to California with her husband several years ago. Charlie—well, he's unemployed, unmotivated, and I'm not sure what to do for him. I'd like to encourage him to get a job by promising that, when Barbara passes away, he can own the farm for the rest of his life if he has obtained employment beforehand and if he keeps his job afterward. But, in the long run, whether Charlie gets a job or not, I want Debbie to end up with the farm. She has several kids, and I'm sure she or one of her kids would be responsible enough to keep the farm in the family. Can you fix my will to accomplish these goals? Oh—one more thing. Debbie doesn't get along with Charlie at all. I think she would do anything to keep him from living there. In fact, when she visited over Christmas last year, I heard her telling Barbara that very thing. And Barbara, she's so close to Debbie—she would do anything for her. . . . I'm not sure you can do anything about it, but I thought I would let you know.

What should you discuss with Anna? How should you draft the provision in Anna's will devising Meadowacre?

CHAPTER 8

NON-DESTRUCTIBLE CONTINGENT REMAINDERS; THE RAP AND EXECUTORY INTERESTS

▪ ▪ ▪

A. NON-DESTRUCTIBILITY—CONTINGENT REMAINDERS CAN TRANSFORM INTO EXECUTORY INTERESTS

Most states have abolished the doctrine of destructibility of contingent remainders. If contingent remainders are not destructible, they cannot be destroyed either for failure to vest in time or by merger or renunciation. (However, it is still possible that a contingent remainder will never vest—if the condition precedent is never met or the unascertained owner is never born or never meets the definition of ownership.)

To understand the implications of eliminating the destructibility rule, consider the following conveyance and subsequent factual developments:

O to A for life, then if B marries C, to B (B has not married C)

A owns a life estate, B owns a contingent remainder in fee, and O has retained a reversion. The contingent remainder is valid under the RAP because the condition precedent—that B marry C—can only be satisfied while B and C are both alive and thus will be finally tested when one of them dies, making B and C validating lives. If contingent remainders are destructible, A is also a validating life, because the remainder will be destroyed if it does not vest by the expiration of A's life estate. If contingent remainders are not destructible, B and C do not have to marry before A dies in order for B to take possession of the property, so A is not a validating life. But the remainder is still valid because only one validating life is required, and here we have two, B and C.

What if O later sells his reversion to A but B has still not married C? On the face of things, A owns a life estate, B owns a contingent remainder in fee, and A owns a reversion. If contingent remainders are destructible, we merge A's two interests into a fee and destroy B's remainder. If contingent remainders are not destructible, we do not merge A's two interests and thus do not destroy B's remainder, leaving the state of the title as it is on its face, with A now owning both the life estate and reversion bracketing B's contingent remainder. What if A then dies and B has still not married C? If contingent remainders are destructible, A's fee would pass to his devisee or heir. If contingent remainders are not destructible, B's interest can continue even though it did not vest by the expiration of the preceding estate. A's life estate expires, but B cannot take possession because he has not satisfied the condition precedent of marrying C. The next non-contingent interest, the reversion, becomes possessory, and, given that A died, that interest is now owned by A's devisee or heir. A reversion is presumptively in fee, but here that fee is defeasible based on the condition regarding B marrying C; A's devisee or heir therefore owns a fee subject to an executory limitation. Because B's interest no longer follows an expirable estate but instead now can cut off a fee, B's contingent remainder becomes an executory interest following the fee subject to an executory limitation. It is a springing executory interest because it follows what was a reversion, an interest originally retained by the grantor. A's devisee/heir therefore now owns a fee subject to an executory limitation, and B now owns a springing executory interest in fee.

If B later marries C, the property will spring to B in fee simple. If B or C dies and they have never married, A's devisee or heir will then own a fee simple, because the executory limitation of B marrying C will never be met.

In Chapter 3, we learned that a reversion always follows a contingent remainder. Reconsider this example from that chapter:

O to A for life, then to B if B marries C, otherwise to D (B has not married C)

A owns a life estate, B owns a contingent remainder in fee, and D owns an alternative contingent remainder in fee. If contingent remainders are not destructible, is there still a need for O to retain a reversion? Consider what will occur if A dies, B and C are still alive, and B has not yet married C: A's life estate expires, and the next non-contingent interest must take possession. Here, neither B's nor D's remainder is vested—B's remainder has not vested because he has not married C, and D's remainder has not vested because it is still possible that B could marry C (in other words, it is not yet the case that B never married C). O therefore still retained a reversion to cover this possibility. Because neither remainder is vested, B and D are not entitled to possession when A dies, and the property reverts to O. Most jurisdictions that have abolished destructibility have done so by statute, and the resulting classification of interests will be governed by that statute or state common law and may vary. The most natural reading of the state of the title at A's death would be as if O had conveyed the property as follows:

O to B when B marries C, but if B does not marry C, then to D

O would thus own a fee subject to an executory limitation, B would own a springing executory interest in fee, and D also would own a springing executory interest in fee (D's interest might more accurately be labeled an alternative springing executory interest in fee, although that terminology was not used at common law).

B. THE RAP AND EXECUTORY INTERESTS

You were first introduced to the RAP in Chapter 4, where you learned how it applies to contingent and class remainders. The RAP also applies to executory interests. ***The RAP only applies to contingent remainders, remainders to a class of persons, and executory interests—it does not invalidate any other interest!*** The RAP is misnamed—the rule was not designed to eliminate *all* perpetuities, but only potentially perpetual contingent remainders, class remainders, and executory interests. Consider for example:

O to A and his heirs as long as the land is farmed

A has a fee simple determinable and O has a possibility of reverter. The condition is potentially perpetual—the timeframe during which the land could stop being farmed is indefinite—and yet the RAP does not apply to this grant, because the RAP does not apply to any future interest the grantor retains, including possibilities of reverter. By contrast, if O instead creates an executory interest following the same present estate,

O to A and his heirs as long as the land is farmed, then to B

the executory interest is potentially perpetual and void under the RAP. Once it is invalidated, O has, by operation of law, retained a (potentially perpetual) possibility of reverter; hence the misnomer.

Let's consider in depth how the RAP applies to executory interests. Recall the sequence of analysis you learned in Chapter 4. First, analyze the state of the title at the time of the grant. Then, determine if there is a contingent remainder, a class interest, or, now, an executory interest. If so, then test the interest to see if it withstands the RAP, which you strictly and remorselessly apply.

Remember the traditional phrasing of the rule: "No interest is good unless it must vest, if at all, within 21 years of a life in being at the creation of the interest." For an executory interest, "vest" is imprecise, because there are no "contingent" or "vested" executory interests. For an executory interest, "vest" means ***become a present estate (possessory)***. As with a contingent remainder, however, you do not have to guarantee that the executory interest

> For an executory interest to survive the RAP, you must be able to guarantee that, within 21 years after all lives in being have died, the interest will either become possessory or no longer exist.

will vest—in this case, become possessory. Instead, *if* the executory interest ***will vest, it must be guaranteed to do so*** within 21 years of a life in being. In other words, ***an executory interest cannot exist as an executory interest indefinitely; it must be certain either to become possessory or to no longer exist within the RAP period, and it is void if there is any possibility it will still be an executory interest (i.e., not yet a present possessory estate) more than 21 years after all lives in being at the time the interest was created have died***. If you can guarantee that an executory interest will either become possessory or no longer exist within 21 years of the lifetime/death of someone alive at the time of the grant (particularly, anyone named in the deed or will), you have a validating life and the executory interest is valid under the RAP. If not, the executory interest is void.

Reconsider the example above:

O to A and his heirs as long as the land is farmed, then to B

You must test to see if B's executory interest could remain an executory interest longer than 21 years after all lives in being have died. You do not have to guarantee that B's executory interest will become a present estate; rather, for the interest to be valid under the RAP, you must be able to guarantee that B's interest cannot be an executory interest indefinitely. If B's interest becomes possessory, it must do so within 21 years of some life in being. Here, the owner of the property could stop farming the land at any time in the indefinite future, and thus there is no validating life. Because B's interest is invalid, we strike it, leaving:

O to A and his heirs as long as the land is farmed

B loses his executory interest and O retains a possibility of reverter (demonstrating yet again that the RAP is misnamed—it does not invalidate all perpetuities, including O's potentially perpetual possibility of reverter).

Compare this example:

O to A and his heirs, but if the land ceases to be farmed, then to B

This grant is substantively the same as the one above but structurally different, with A owning a fee subject to an executory limitation and B owning a shifting executory interest in fee. For the same reasons as above, the condition—and the executory interest—are potentially perpetual, there is no validating life, and B's executory interest is invalid. How much of the original language do we strike? If we strike only the executory interest ("then to B"), we would be left with

O to A and his heirs, but if the land ceases to be farmed,

which makes no sense. Whenever the potentially perpetual condition precedes the void executory interest and is set off from it, you must strike both the condition and the invalid interest. Thus, here we strike

O to A and his heirs, ~~but if the land ceases to be farmed, then to B~~

leaving

O to A and his heirs

Because of the RAP, A now owns a fee.

Compare another example:

O to A and his heirs as long as A farms the land, then to B

In this case, the defeasance clause is expressly tied directly to A's life, and so B's shifting executory interest must either become possessory or cease to exist by A's death. A is therefore the validating life, and B's executory interest is valid.

As with contingent remainders, a savings clause can be used to make an executory interest valid under the RAP. For example:

O to A and his heirs as long as the land is farmed, then to B and his heirs, if B is then living

A owns a fee simple determinable and B owns a shifting executory interest in fee. If the conveyance ended at "then to B and his heirs," the executory interest would not be tied to any life in being, would be potentially perpetual (the land could cease being farmed at any point), and thus would be void under the RAP. This savings clause preserves the executory interest by tying the condition that precedes the interest to B's lifetime, making B the validating life.

C. HOW THE RAP CAN AFFECT OTHER INTERESTS

Although the RAP does not apply to any interests other than contingent remainders, class interests, and executory interests, it can **affect** other interests. For example, consider this conveyance:

O to A for life, then to B and his heirs, but if state-sponsored prayer returns to public schools, then to C and his heirs

On the face of the grant, A owns a life estate; it is not defeasible because the state-sponsored prayer condition is not immediately after A's life interest, nor is it explicitly applicable to it. B's interest is a remainder, because it immediately follows a life interest. It is vested because B is ascertainable and there is no condition precedent, and because it is vested, the RAP does not apply to it. There is, however, a condition subsequent to B's remainder. Because state-sponsored prayer could return to public schools either before or after B's remainder becomes possessory, B owns a vested remainder, subject to divestment, in fee subject to an executory limitation. C's interest is not a remainder because it does not immediately follow an expirable interest—it can cut off B's interest—and thus it is an executory interest. It is shifting because, if C takes possession, he will do so by cutting off an interest owned by another grantee in the original grant, B. C thus owns a shifting executory interest in fee.

The RAP must be applied to the executory interest. It is not certain that state-sponsored prayer will return to the public schools within 21 years of the life of some life in being (here, O, A, B or C). Because this condition is potentially perpetual and not tied to any life in being, the executory interest could exist indefinitely as an executory interest and thus is void under the RAP. As explained above, we must strike both the executory interest and the condition, leaving:

O to A for life, then to B and his heirs

The result is A owns a life estate and B owns a vested remainder in fee. Even though the RAP did not **apply to** B's vested remainder, it did **affect** it; indeed, the RAP expanded B's vested remainder, making it indefeasible and fully vested, no longer subject to divestment.

D. ELIMINATION OF DESTRUCTIBILITY AND RESULTING RAP ISSUES

As we learned at the beginning of this chapter, most states have eliminated the doctrine of destructibility of contingent remainders, and thus a contingent remainder can continue, as an executory interest, beyond the expiration of the preceding estate. The elimination of destructibility allows some remainders to continue that would otherwise be destroyed, but it also has the consequence of making some contingent remainders void under the RAP.

Consider this conveyance:

O to A for life, then if B marries C, to B (B has not married C)

A owns a life estate, B owns a contingent remainder (condition precedent not yet fulfilled) in fee, and O has retained a reversion. Assuming contingent remainders are not destructible, and B has not married C by A's death, O's reversion will then become possessory as a fee subject to an executory limitation, and B's remainder will become a springing executory interest in fee. B's interest is still valid under the RAP, because B and C must both be alive for them to marry, and thus they are the validating lives. If they never marry, B's interest will never vest and will cease to exist once either B or C dies. If B and C marry after A's death, at that time the fee will spring to B.

Contrast this example:

O to A for life, then if state-sponsored prayer returns to public schools, to B

A owns a life estate, B owns a contingent remainder (condition precedent not yet fulfilled) in fee, and O has retained a reversion. We must apply the RAP to B's contingent remainder. If destructibility applies, the contingent remainder is valid, because B's remainder must vest by A's death or it will be destroyed for failure to vest in time, making A the validating life. The destructibility rule thus limited the potential contingency of remainders and avoided a RAP problem. If, on the other hand, contingent remainders are not destructible, B's remainder does not have to vest by A's death and can theoretically continue as an executory interest. Given that B's interest is in fee, his interest could continue on indefinitely, more than 21 years after all lives in being (O, A, and B) have died. In other words, it is not certain that, if state-sponsored prayer returns to public schools, it must do so within 21 years of the lifetime (death) of either O, A, or B. B's contingent remainder and the condition precedent to it are therefore void from inception, leaving A with a life estate and O with a reversion. The destructibility rule limited the applicability of the condition precedent to A's lifetime and thus preserved B's remainder up to A's death, while the elimination of destructibility leads to B's remainder being void under the RAP.

CHAPTER 8 SUMMARY

The RAP applies *only* to contingent remainders, class remainders, and executory interests. However, the RAP can affect other interests.

For an executory interest to survive the RAP, you must be able to guarantee that the executory interest must become possessory or cease to exist (i.e., no longer be an executory interest) within 21 years of a life in being.

If contingent remainders are not destructible, and if a valid contingent remainder does not vest by the expiration of the preceding estate, then the contingent remainder becomes an executory interest. Some contingent remainders that were valid under the RAP due to the destructibility rule may be invalid if contingent remainders are no longer destructible.

E. PRACTICE PROBLEMS

Answer problem 1.

1.   To what interests does the RAP apply?

Provide the state of title on the face of the grant for problems 2–7. Test any executory interests under the RAP, and then provide the state of title after applying the RAP.

2.   O to A until any of O's children reach 18, then to B.

3.   O to A, but if A's heir or devisee opens a restaurant on the premises, then to B.

4.   T devises Blackacre to A, but if T's children ever become destitute, then to those children.

5.   O to A as long as any of O's children are alive and not older than 21, then to B (O has one child, C, who is 9).

6.   O to A, but if chickens are ever raised on the property, then O may enter and reclaim the property.

7.   O to A, but if any of O's children ever go on a mission trip to the Philippines, then to those children.

For problems 8–10, provide the state of title at the time of the grant and after each stated event. Assume contingent remainders are not destructible.

8.   O conveys Blackacre to A for life, then one year later to B. Several years after the conveyance, A dies.

9.   O conveys Blackacre to A for life, then to B if B ever attends Harvard. Years later, when A dies, B still has not attended Harvard. However, two years after A's death, B attends Harvard.

10. O conveys Blackacre to A for life, then to B for life if B outlives O, then to C two years after either A's, B's, or O's death (whichever comes latest). Five years after the conveyance, B dies. Two years later, O dies. Finally, A dies.

Putting it together: Provide the state of title (both before and after the RAP) for the conveyances in problems 11–18. Assume that the Rule in Shelley's Case and the Doctrine of Worthier Title apply. If it makes a difference whether contingent remainders are destructible, then provide both answers.

11. O to A for life, then to B, but if anyone ever builds a factory on the premises, then to C.

12. O to A in fee tail, then to B as long as corn is grown on the property, then to C.

13. T devises Blackacre to A for life, then to T's children, but if any of T's grandchildren climb Mt. Everest, then to the first grandchild to do so (T has two children at her death).

14. O to A, but if a person ever walks on Mars, then to B.

15. O to A for life, then to B if a person walks on Mars.

16. O to A as long as the house on the premises remains standing, then to B.

17. T devises Blackacre to A, but if any of T's children survive A, then to those children.

18. O to A for life, then to B for life, then to B's youngest child for life, then if B's youngest child's heirs are adults, to that child's heirs.

Provide the state of title (both before and after the RAP, and at each factual development along the way) for the conveyances in problems 19 and 20. Assume that the Rule in Shelley's Case and the Doctrine of Worthier Title apply. If it makes a difference whether contingent remainders are destructible, or whether there is a statute of limitations on Possibilities of Reverter and Rights of Entry, then provide alternative answers.

19. O to A for life, then to A's children who reach age 20 for life, then to B, but if O has a grandchild who reaches 20, then at that time to that grandchild (O has one child, C, who is 10, and A has no children).

    a.   Five years after the grant, A has a child, D.

    b.   Three years after D is born, A dies.

    c.   25 years after the grant, D turns 20.

    d.   Twenty years after D turns 20, C's first child, E, turns 20.

20. O to A for life as long as A lives in Virginia, then to B for life as long as B lives in Virginia.

    a.   A lives in Virginia for 35 years, then moves to New Hampshire. B does not live in Virginia when A moves to New Hampshire.

    b.   5 years after A moves to New Hampshire, B moves to Virginia.

Answer problem 21.

21. Oliver is a diehard fan of the newest NFL team, the England Tories, and has a house one block away from Schick Stadium, the venue where the Tories play "home" games in the U.S. Oliver has to move away for a job and wants his best friend, Alex, who is also a Tories fan, to have the house for his lifetime so he can easily attend Tories' games. But Oliver wants the house back if the Tories no longer play at Schick Stadium. Oliver's other friend Bill is a fan of quarterback Tom Trelow, so if Trelow helps the Tories win the Super Bowl, Oliver wants Bill to have the house. He thinks he can handle the transfer without an attorney, so he drafts the following conveyance: "I, Oliver, convey my House near Schick Stadium to Alex for his lifetime as long as the Tories play at Schick Stadium. Otherwise, the House will become mine again and I will have the right to reclaim it. If the Tories win the Super Bowl while Tom Trelow is on the team, then at that time my house will belong to Bill." Has Oliver accomplished his goals? What is the state of the title?

F. CLASS DISCUSSION PROBLEMS

Provide the state of title (before and after the RAP) for the conveyances in the following problems. Assume that the Rule in Shelley's Case and the Doctrine of Worthier Title apply. If it makes a difference whether contingent remainders are destructible, then provide both answers.

1. O to A, but if any of O's children graduate high school, then to those graduates.

2. O to A as long as A does not join the Bird-Watching Society, then to B for life, then to O's youngest son.

3. O to A for life, then to B if B has more than five grandchildren (B has no grandchildren).

4. O to A for life, then to B if B has passed the bar exam, otherwise to O's heirs.

5. T devises Blackacre to A for life, then to A's children for life, then to B if T never has grandchildren, otherwise to T's grandchildren (A has no children and T has no grandchildren).

6. O to A for life, then to B, but if O's widow ever remarries, then to C.

7. T devises Blackacre to A for life, then to B if B survives T's children.

8. O to A, but if all of O's children reach age 21, then to B.

9. O to A, but if any of O's grandchildren reach age 10, then to the first grandchild to do so (O has one grandchild who is nine years old).

10. O to A for life, then to A's youngest child for life, then to A's youngest descendant alive at A's death.

11. O to A for life, then to O's children for life, then to B in fee (O has no children).

    a.   10 years later A dies, and O has no children.

    b.   3 years after A dies, O's first child is born.

For problem 12, assume that contingent remainders are destructible and that a statute of limitations allows rights of entry and possibilities of reverter to exist for only 30 years. Analyze the state of title both at the time of the devise and after each subsequent factual development.

12. Linda owns Whiteacre in fee. She drafts a will leaving Whiteacre "to my son—Alfred—for life as long as Whiteacre is farmed during the lifetime of my children, then to my son—Brandon—for life, then to my youngest daughter—Clara—for life if she marries a farmer, then to my cousin Donald in fee simple absolute." Linda dies in 2021. Alfred diligently farms the property until 2053 when he sustains serious injuries in a car accident. No other family member continues farm operations on Whiteacre thereafter. Sadly, Alfred's age and his injuries weaken him, and he dies in 2054. Many of Alfred's family and friends come to his funeral. His sister, Clara, brings her first (and only) husband—an engineer—and her children. Brandon and Donald also attend. While they visit afterwards, Donald decides to sell his interest in Whiteacre to Brandon. They draft the appropriate documents and complete the sale on the same day.

CHAPTER 9

OTHER MODERN REFORMS AND COMPLEXITIES

■ ■ ■

A. THE ABOLITION OF THE FEE TAIL

Only a few states still recognize the fee tail. In those states, as we learned in Chapter 2, the fee tail may be disentailed. The majority of states have abolished the fee tail in one of two ways. Some states treat a conveyance in fee tail as one in fee. Under this approach, the conveyance

O to A and the heirs of his body

will be construed as if it were written

O to A and his heirs

and therefore as a conveyance of a fee.

Other states enforce O's desire to impose a bloodline restriction on A's present estate, but only for one generation. Thus, a fee tail conveyance will be construed as if it were written

O to A and his heirs as long as A dies with a bodily heir

A now owns a fee simple determinable, and O retains a possibility of reverter (until A dies), rather than the reversion that would have followed the fee tail.[1] If A dies without a bodily heir, title will revert to O via the possibility of reverter. If A dies with a bodily heir, then A's devisee or heir will own a fee, and because the bodily heir requirement is only a one time condition, O's possibility of reverter will cease to exist (unlike the reversion that would have continued after the fee tail).

If, rather than retaining a reversion, O conveyed the future interest to a third party, such as

O to A and the heirs of his body, then to B and his heirs

the conveyance will be read as if it says:

O to A and his heirs as long as A dies with a bodily heir,
then to B and his heirs

A thus owns a fee simple determinable, rather than a fee tail, and B owns a shifting executory interest, rather than a vested remainder, in fee.

B. RAP REFORM—THE UNIFORM STATUTORY RULE AGAINST PERPETUITIES (USRAP)

Many states have adopted RAP reforms, with some eliminating or restricting the applicability of the RAP. The most common reform is the Uniform Statutory Rule against Perpetuities (USRAP), which includes three steps:

- First, ***apply the common law rule***; if the interest is valid, then it stands. If the interest would be void under the common law RAP, then proceed to step two:

- Second, ***see whether the terms of the grant expressly guarantee the tested interest must "vest," as defined by the RAP, within 90 years of the interest's***

---

[1] Given that this possibility of reverter is created by law and not by grant, and is expressly limited to A's lifetime, it is unlikely that a statutory limitation on the existence of a possibility of reverter would apply to it, but you would need to consult any applicable state statute for the definitive answer.

creation. Step two essentially requires seeing if there is an explicit wait and see savings clause to that effect, such as:

O to A as long as the property is farmed, then to B if the property is not farmed within 90 years of the date of this conveyance

If the conveyance does not include an explicit limitation of no longer than 90 years, and thus the interest is still not valid, then proceed to step three:

- Third, *wait and see whether the interest <u>in fact</u> "vests," as defined by the RAP, within 90 years of the interest's creation*. A contingent remainder must therefore vest or cease to exist, a class remainder must close or cease to exist, or an executory interest must become possessory or cease to exist, within 90 years of its creation.

All interests that would have been void under the common law RAP are accordingly subject to a wait and see period of up to 90 years, either by an explicit savings clause to that effect (step two) or by operation of law (step three).

C. MODERN COMPLEXITY—LIFE ESTATE VS. FEE

The modern presumption in favor of the fee simple can be overcome by clear evidence of intent to create a lesser estate. Consider this conveyance:

O to A as long as B is alive, then to C

Applying the presumption in favor of the fee, and employing the constructional rule that "as long as" signifies a determinable clause, A would own a fee simple determinable, followed by C's shifting executory interest in fee. But notice that the determinable clause, by its express terms, limits the estate to B's life. Could this be construed, alternatively, as a life estate pur autre vie, followed by a vested remainder in fee? The English common law would have so held because it presumed against a fee, and, in cases of ambiguity, presumed in favor of a remainder over an executory interest. The latter presumption is hardly surprising, given that the common law judges did not recognize executory interests but were forced to accept them by courts of equity and later Parliament via the Statute of Uses. A presumption in favor of a vested remainder would have benefitted C, because, under the English common law, vested remainders were alienable but executory interests were not. Today, given the presumption in favor of a fee, and the free alienability of executory interests, there is no inherent reason to prefer either result; however, because the determinable clause makes it clear A's interest will end at B's death, when C's interest is certain to become possessory, it is arguably most logical to consider this a life estate pur autre vie followed by a vested remainder in fee.

Consider a slight change to the wording of the grant:

O to A as long as B is alive, then to C and his heirs

Here, the fact that the grantor used "and his heirs" for C's interest but not for A's suggests an intent to convey a fee interest to C but a lesser interest—some form of a life estate—to A. This provides even stronger support for the conclusion that A's interest is a life estate for the life of B, leaving C with a vested remainder in fee.

Consider another example:

O to A as long A lives on the land, then to B

This grant is ambiguous. Presumptively, it creates a fee simple determinable followed by a shifting executory interest in fee. However, the grant could be construed to convey to A only a life estate determinable, because A will no longer be farming the land once he dies. O could have more clearly granted a fee to A by drafting the deed like this:

O to A as long A lives on the land until his death, then to B

In this conveyance, there is no ambiguity regarding whether A's interest naturally expires at A's death; indeed, if A continued to live on the property until his death, the condition is fully satisfied, and A's devisee or heirs will own a fee.

Contrast this example:

O to A as long as A does not farm the land, then to B

Although this condition also relates to A's use of the land, because it is a negative condition, A can definitively satisfy it by abstaining from farming until he dies. This grant should be presumed to create a fee simple determinable.

In most cases, the above distinctions will have no relevance in modern law. However, if, for example, the law limited the alienability or the time of existence (e.g., through a statute of limitations) of an executory interest but not a remainder, then the classification could be dispositive. As we have seen, sloppy drafting can lead to unclear titles and unintended outcomes, so in the practice of law, you should take care to be precise in your word choices.

D. REFORMS IN THE RESTATEMENT (3d) OF PROPERTY

The Restatement (3d) of Property streamlines and simplifies the system of present estates and future interests. The fee simple determinable, the fee subject to a condition subsequent, and the fee subject to an executory limitation are combined in the single category "defeasible fee." Similarly, all future interests are combined into two categories: any future interest retained by the grantor is a reversion, and any future interest conveyed to a grantee is a remainder, which is vested if it is certain to become possessory, and is otherwise contingent. Although this system has the laudable benefit of simplicity, it is less precise and has not yet gained acceptance. Property reforms can disrupt records of title and thus most states enact them cautiously. This book will be updated and expanded if and when states embrace the reforms in the Restatement (3d). In the meantime, it is still necessary to master the common law of present estates and future interests. If you master the common law system, you will be able to adjust easily to a more simplified system, but, as you should now fully appreciate, the reverse would not be true.

CHAPTER 9 SUMMARY

Modern approaches to the fee tail:

- Some states have abolished the fee tail, treating a conveyance in fee tail as a fee.
- Other states interpret a fee tail to impose a bloodline restriction on the grantee's estate, but only for one generation.

RAP Reform (the USRAP): Many states have adopted the USRAP, which includes three steps:

- Apply the common law RAP. If the interest would be void under the common law, then:
- Test whether the interest is expressly required to vest within 90 years of the interest's creation. If not, then:
- Wait and see whether the interest in fact vests within 90 years of its creation.

Under modern law, when an ambiguous grant could create either a fee simple determinable followed by an executory interest or a life estate followed by a remainder, the fee simple determinable and executory interest are preferred, absent clear language to the contrary.

E. PRACTICE PROBLEMS

In problems 1 and 2, provide the state of title under every approach to the fee tail.

1. O conveys Blueacre to A and the heirs of her body, but if A uses Blueacre for industrial purposes, then to B.

2. O conveys Redacre to A and the heirs of his body, then to B and his heirs. A subsequently conveys to C and his heirs. Explain fully how you would assess who now owns what interests in Redacre.

Assume that your jurisdiction has adopted the USRAP and applies the Rule in Shelley's Case and the Doctrine of Worthier Title. Provide the state of title for the conveyances in problems 3–11. If it makes a difference whether contingent remainders are destructible, provide both answers.

3. O conveys Blackacre to A for life, then to B if the land is farmed for the next 90 years.

4. O conveys Blackacre to A for life, then to B, but if there is a manned mission to Mars within 80 years, then to the first astronaut to set foot on Mars.

5. O conveys Blackacre to A for life, then to O's grandchildren who reach age 50 (O has no grandchildren).

6. O conveys Blackacre to A in fee tail, then to O's issue alive at the time A's fee tail expires.

7. O conveys Blackacre to A, but if drought prevents the land from being farmed, then O may enter and reclaim Blackacre.

8. O conveys Blackacre to A, but if A or A's issue ever runs for public office, then to B, if B is then living.

9. O conveys Blackacre to A for life, then to B if B has grandchildren, otherwise to C (B has no grandchildren).

10. O conveys Blackacre to A for life, then to B when B adopts A's children.

11. O conveys Blackacre to A as long as B lives, then to C.

F. CLASS DISCUSSION PROBLEMS

For problems 1 and 2, provide the state of title under every approach to the fee tail. Assume your jurisdiction follows the Doctrine of Worthier Title.

1. O conveys Mapleacre to A for life, then to B and the heirs of her body, then to C.

2. O conveys Redacre to A in fee tail, but if O's heirs are willing to farm the property, then to O's heirs.

Assume that your jurisdiction has adopted the USRAP and applies the Rule in Shelley's Case and the Doctrine of Worthier Title. Provide the state of title for the conveyances in problems 3–10. If it makes a difference whether contingent remainders are destructible, provide both answers.

3. O conveys Blackacre to A when O's last child graduates high school.

4. O conveys Blackacre to A for life, then to B for life, then to C, but if anyone opens a grocery store on the premises, then at that time to D.

5. O conveys Blackacre to A for life, then for life to A's children who join the Navy, then to B.

6. O conveys Blackacre to A for life, then to B if B is then living, otherwise to A's heirs.

7. O conveys Blackacre to A for life, then to B, but if anyone uses the land for cattle grazing during the next 90 years, then at that time to Western State University.

8. O conveys Blackacre to A for life, then to B as long as the land is never strip-mined.

9. O conveys Blackacre to A for life, then to A's children for life, then to O's children who outlive all of A's children (A has one child, B).

10. O conveys Blackacre to A as long as A remains employed, then if B marries C, to B.

For problem 11, assume that your jurisdiction follows the USRAP and contingent remainders are not destructible. Analyze the state of title both at the time of the grant and after each subsequent factual development.

11. In 1958, Carter conveyed Redacre to his brother—Ryan—for life effective when Ryan gets married, then to Ryan's first-born child for life, then to Ryan's grandchildren in fee, but if the land is used for commercial purposes, then at that time to Carter's other brother, Bob. Ryan married Christy in 1961. In 1963, Ryan and Christy had their first child, Allen. In 1968, they had another child, Brianna. Ryan died in 1990. Allen, who never married or had children, died of cancer in 2000. Brianna did not marry until 2003, and she had her first child, Jonathan, in 2004. Until 2010—when a hotel was opened on Redacre—the premises were only used for residential purposes.

Problem 12: Solving a crime.

12. One evening, you turn on the local news, which is covering a recent murder. Donna Jones, the daughter of a prominent businessman, had been found dead the day before her wedding, but the police did not yet have any leads regarding who committed the crime. Tired—and not wanting to hear anything more—you change the channel, little suspecting that the police would soon be seeking your advice during the investigation.

The following morning, a friend—Officer Tom Brown—stops by your law office. According to Tom, they still have no suspects, though they had found a hastily scribbled (and anonymous) note at the crime scene. The note read in part, "You finally got what was coming to you, and I get the family estate after all."

"The funny thing is," says Tom, "both her father and her uncle appear to have left the land to her in their wills. I've brought a number of wills and documents. Would you mind looking at them to see if you can come up with anything?"

"Sure," you say as you open a manila folder. The first document, a will written for Stephen Jones (Tom tells you Stephen, now deceased, was Donna's grandfather, and that Stephen had four children), contains a sentence stating, "I leave the Jones estate to my son Andrew, but if anyone uses the land for commercial instead of residential purposes, then my other son Robert and the heirs of his body may own and possess the estate."

Seeing little of immediate interest in the will, you put it down and turn to the next, which is Andrew's will: "I, Andrew Jones, hereby devise all my land holdings to my son, Charles, but if Charles dies before reaching age 30, then my niece Donna will own the property."

The mention of Donna piques your interest, but finding little other substance in the will, you turn to the third document. It is a will written by Robert, which reads, "I leave all of my real estate to my only child, Donna, and the heirs of her body. I leave all my other interests to my nephew Nicholas."

After thinking a few moments, you ask Tom, "Donna was about to get married, right? Did she already have any kids?"

"No," Tom replies. "But we did check to see what land Donna owned. Apparently, the only land she has is an estate that her grandfather owned—it has been in the Jones family for years."

You reply, "Well, based on these documents, I might have someone for you to investigate. But first, let me do some quick research to confirm what approach our state takes on a couple of legal issues."

Whom do you most suspect of killing Donna? What do you want to know about the law applicable in your jurisdiction? Why?

CHAPTER 10

ADDITIONAL PRACTICE PROBLEMS

■ ■ ■

Problems 1–16 include an initial conveyance, and some then provide a series of subsequent factual developments. Analyze the state of the title at the time of the grant and then at each point in the chronological chain of events. If necessary, apply the common law RAP. Explain at each point if your answer depends on different approaches to a relevant legal concept.

1. O to D for life as long as she remains single, then upon D's death to S and his heirs.
   a. At the time of the grant, D and S are alive; D is single.

   b. D marries.

   c. D dies.

2. O to A for life, then to B for life if B marries C, then to A's heirs.

3. O to J as long as an Eastern State University graduate is not selected to serve as President of Western State University, then to A and her heirs (an ESU graduate has never been selected to serve as President of WSU).

4. O to A when communism collapses in North Korea.

5. O to A for life, then to B and his heirs, but if B fails to live to 50, then to C and his heirs (B is 10).

6. O to A for the life of Q, then to B and his heirs if B marries C.
   a. At the time of the grant, B is unmarried.

   b. O sells his remaining interest in Blackacre to A.

95

7. O to A for life, then to B and his heirs, but if the land is ever used for commercial purposes, then to Royal University and its successors and assigns.

8. O to A for life, then to B and his heirs so long as the land is not used for commercial purposes, then to Royal University and its successors and assigns.

9. O to A for life, then if a person walks on Mars, to B and his heirs.

10. O to A for life, then to B's first-born child for life, then if Texas has seceded from the union, to C and his heirs. Analyze this grant under two alternative factual scenarios:
    a. At the time of the grant, B has children.

    b. At the time of the grant, B does not have children.

11. O to A for life, then to B as long as B farms Blackacre.

12. O to A for life, then to B if B maintained the property for A.

13. O to A in fee tail, then to B for life if B marries C, then to D.

14. O to A for life, then to B for life, then to C, but if C lives alone on the property, then to O.

15. O to A for life, but if A stops attending church every Sunday, then to B for life, then if C ever attends church, to C.

16. O to A as long as any of O's children are alive and younger than 21, then to B (O has one child, C, who is 9).

For problems 17–18, first give the state of title on the face of the grant. Identify any interests that are threatened by the RAP. Test the interests, and give the state of title after applying the RAP. Apply the Rule in Shelley's Case as applicable. Assume contingent remainders are not destructible.

17. O to A for life, then to O's last daughter to graduate college (O is 90 years old; she has five children, all of whom have graduated college; Z was the most recent daughter to so graduate).

18. O to A for life, then to B if B's grandchildren graduate high school (none of B's grandchildren have yet graduated high school).

Determine the state of title after each event in problem 19. If you do not have enough information to determine the state of title after every event, explain why.

19. O conveys Blackacre to A for life, then to B as long as the property is used during B's lifetime for residential purposes. After A dies, B begins residing on the sprawling estate. Nonetheless, sensing economic opportunity when the population in a nearby city expands, B develops Blackacre and turns it into a shopping center.

Problems 20–24 build on concepts you have already learned, testing how deeply you can analyze their implications. These problems are difficult, and do not be surprised if you cannot determine the answers. Determine the state of title.

20. O to A for life, then to B for life if B is then an adult, then to A's heirs as long as O does not die before O's children reach adulthood, then to O's heirs.

21. O conveys Greenacre to A and his heirs in fee simple for his lifetime.

22. T devises Blackacre to A for life, then to T's children if they reach age 20 (T has three children, B, C, and D, but only B has reached age 20 by the time T dies). Before C or D reach 20, they—along with A—drown in the storm surge of a category 5 hurricane. Only B survives. (Hint: do you see the ambiguity?).

23. T writes a will leaving Blackacre to A for life, then to A's heirs. A dies. Then T dies.

24. O grants Blackacre to A while A is living, but if A dies O may enter and reclaim.

CHAPTER 11

ANSWERS TO CHAPTER PRACTICE PROBLEMS

■ ■ ■

CHAPTER 2

For problems 1–4, identify which attributes of property rights are associated with each property interest (*the next chapter will provide more information on the attributes of a remainder*).

1. Fee simple absolute: The fee is the ultimate interest in realty, and so all attributes of property rights come with it. The fee is alienable, devisable, and inheritable.

2. Life estate: The life estate is <u>only</u> alienable for the owner's life (i.e., by creating a life estate pur autre vie). The life estate is generally not inheritable or devisable. However, at modern law, the life estate pur autre vie is devisable and inheritable (but only as long as the measuring life lives). At common law, the life estate pur autre vie was also devisable and inheritable <u>if</u> the original conveyance explicitly indicated so (e.g., "O to A <u>and his heirs</u> for the life of B").

3. Fee tail: At common law, the fee tail was only alienable for the owner's life (i.e., as a life estate pur autre vie). By definition, the fee tail is not devisable because it must go to the grantee's bodily heirs. The only exception is if A—the owner of the fee tail—conveys a life estate for his own life to another party. As long as A still lives, B can devise the life estate pur autre vie. Finally, the fee tail is inheritable, but only by bodily heirs.

4. Reversion: The reversion is alienable, inheritable, and devisable.

Answer problem 5.

5. Name the expirable estates and the two types of future interests that patiently follow them.

   The expirable estates are the life estate and the fee tail. They are immediately (patiently) followed by either a reversion (in the grantor) or a remainder (in a grantee).

For problems 6–10, read the conveyance, identify the words of purchase, the words of limitation, and the present estate granted to A (remember, O is presumed to own a fee simple absolute).

6. O conveys Blackacre "to A and his heirs."
   a. Words of purchase: "to A"
   b. Words of limitation: "and his heirs"
   c. A's present estate: Fee simple absolute

7. O conveys Blackacre "to A and his bodily heirs."
   a. Words of purchase: "to A"
   b. Words of limitation: "and his bodily heirs"
   c. A's present estate: Fee tail

8. O conveys Blackacre "to A for life."
   a. Words of purchase: "to A"
   b. Words of limitation: "for life"
   c. A's present estate: Life estate

9. O conveys Blackacre "to A."

    a. Words of purchase: "to A"

    b. Words of limitation: None, but at modern law, specific words of limitation are not necessary to convey a fee; O is presumed to convey his full fee, absent clear intent to the contrary.

    c. A's present estate: Fee simple absolute

10. O conveys Blackacre "to A for the life of B."

    a. Words of purchase: "to A"

    b. Words of limitation: "for the life of B"

    c. A's present estate: Life estate pur autre vie

For problems 11–18, read the conveyance and determine whether—if at all—A's estate is followed by a reversion or a remainder.

11. O to A for life.

    O: Reversion

12. O to A and his bodily heirs, then to B.

    B: Remainder in fee simple absolute

13. O to A and his heirs.

    Because A has a fee—"full" title—there is no future interest following it, and thus there is no reversion or remainder.

14. O to A and his bodily heirs, then after one year to B.

    Because B's interest does not immediately follow A's fee tail, it is not a remainder. O retains what he doesn't convey, and thus O retains a reversion (for the one year between the expiration of A's fee tail and B's interest; we will study in Chapter 6 how to classify both O's and B's interests more precisely).

15. O to A in fee tail.

    O: Reversion

16. O to A for life, then to B.

    B: Remainder in fee simple absolute

17. O to A, but if A starts smoking, then at that time to B.

    B's interest does not follow naturally after A's estate. Instead, it cuts off A's fee. Because B's interest does not wait patiently, it is not a remainder. O did not retain a reversion because A has a fee interest, not an expirable estate (life estate or fee tail). We will see later how to classify both A's and B's interests more precisely, but for now, you should see that B's interest is not a remainder.

18. O to A in fee tail. A subsequently conveys "to B in fee."

    At the time of the grant:
    O: Reversion

    After A conveys to B in fee:
    O owns nothing because A's conveyance to B disentailed the fee tail, vesting B with fee.

For problems 19–21, read the conveyance or series of conveyances and identify the state of title (i.e., list all of the property interests and who owns them). If there is a series of conveyances or events, identify the state of title after each conveyance or event.

19. O conveys Greenacre to A and his bodily heirs. A then devises Greenacre to his best friend, B, and his heirs. A has no bodily heirs at his death.

    At the time of O's original conveyance, the state of title is:

    A: Fee tail

    O: Reversion

    Although the law in modern jurisdictions that retain a fee tail would allow A to disentail his present estate by conveying it in fee to B, this rule only applies by grant, <u>not</u> by devise. *Therefore, when A dies without a bodily heir*:

    O: Fee simple absolute

20. A executes a will devising Blackacre, which he does not yet own, to B for life, then to C in fee. O then conveys Blackacre to A. A then dies.

    A's will is not effective until A's death, and it doesn't matter that A did not own Blackacre when he wrote the will, as long as A owns Blackacre when he dies. Because O conveyed Blackacre to A before A died, *the state of title when O conveyed to A was*:

    A: Fee simple absolute

    At A's death, A's will takes effect:

    B: Life estate

    C: Remainder in fee simple absolute

21. O conveys Blackacre to A in fee simple, then to B for life.

    The conveyance to B is impossible because A's fee will not naturally expire. Therefore, B owns nothing. Obviously, a drafting error of some sort was committed. Should we construe the grant to give A an expirable interest so that B's remainder is valid? No, because in ambiguous grants, the law favors fee to lesser interests, and in this case the specific grant to A is not even facially ambiguous.

    A: Fee simple absolute (B owns nothing)

CHAPTER 3

For problems 1–2, identify which attributes of property rights are associated with each property interest.

1. Vested remainder

   If the vested remainder still exists, it is alienable, devisable, and inheritable.

2. Contingent remainder

   At common law, contingent remainders were inheritable and devisable but not alienable. Modern law (which is followed in most states) makes contingent remainders alienable.

Answer problems 3–5.

3. What are the characteristics of a vested remainder?

> A vested remainder is owned by a born and ascertained person and not subject to a condition precedent. Obviously—but very importantly—because a vested remainder is a *remainder*, it is a future interest that *waits patiently* until the prior interest *naturally* expires.

4. Under the common law, what are the three ways in which a contingent remainder can be destroyed?

> First, a contingent remainder is destroyed if it does not vest before the prior estate naturally expires. Second, a contingent remainder is destroyed by merger (i.e., the combination of an expirable estate and either a reversion or a vested remainder in fee). Finally, a contingent remainder is destroyed if the preceding expirable estate is renounced.

5. What interests do reversions follow?

> The grantor retains a reversion following a naturally expirable estate (life estate or fee tail) if the grantor does not also convey—in the same grant—the future interest following the expirable estate to a grantee. The grantor also retains a reversion if the last interest the grantor conveyed is a contingent remainder or an alternative contingent remainder, even if on the face of the grant it looks like there is quantum without the reversion (this is because of the doctrine of destructibility).

For problems 6–16, identify if there is a remainder and, if so, whether it is vested, contingent, or vested subject to open. Further classify any remainder by what present estate it will be when it becomes possessory (e.g., fee, fee tail, or life estate).

6. O to A for life, then to B for life.

> B: Vested remainder in a life estate

7. O to A for life, then to B's children in fee simple (B does not yet have any children).

> B's children: Contingent remainder in fee simple absolute (unascertained owner)

8. O to A for life, then to B's children in fee simple (B's first child was born yesterday).

> B's first child: Vested remainder, subject to open, in fee (owner ascertained but others may later meet the definition of ownership)

9. O to A in fee simple absolute, but if A ever raises pigs on the land, then to B.

> B does not have a remainder. A owns the property in fee, and a fee does not naturally expire. Therefore, in order for B to acquire the property, B's interest must cut A's interest short. Remainders always wait patiently. We will learn in Chapter 6 what interest B has.

10. O to A and the heirs of his body, then if B buys a Ferrari, to B and his heirs (B has not bought a Ferrari).

> B: Contingent remainder in fee (condition precedent not yet fulfilled)

11. O to A in fee tail, then to B if B buys a Ferrari (B just bought a Ferrari).

> B: Vested remainder in fee (condition precedent fulfilled, with owner ascertained)

12. O to A for life, then to A's children who reach age 21 *if* they have graduated high school. Consider the following alternative fact patterns:

   a. A has one child, B, who is 17. B is a junior in high school.

   > This remainder is contingent for two reasons. First, its owner is not yet ascertained (none of A's children meet the definition of ownership because none have reached 21). Second, there is an unfulfilled condition precedent ("if they have graduated high school").

   > *Therefore:*

   > A's children who reach age 21: Contingent remainder in fee

   b. A has one child, B, who is 19. B graduated high school.

   > The remainder is still to an unascertained group. Even though B has satisfied the condition precedent, he is not yet 21 and does not meet the ownership criteria (is not part of the specified "class").

   > *Therefore*:

   > A's children who reach age 21: Contingent remainder in fee.

   c. A has one child, B, who just turned 21. B graduated high school.

   > B is now an ascertained member of the class (A's children who reach age 21) who has satisfied the condition precedent.

   > *Therefore*:

   > B: Vested remainder, subject to open, in fee (subject to open because other children of B could still meet the criteria for ownership).

   d. A has two children, B and C. B is 23, and he just graduated high school. C just turned 21, and he already graduated high school.

   > This question raises an ambiguity in the grant. Does it require A's children merely to reach age 21 and *at some time* graduate high school, or does it require them to graduate high school by age 21? Given that the "have graduated high school" clause is directly connected to the requirement of turning 21, a court will probably determine that the clause is meant to require a child to turn 21 and have graduated high school by then.

   > *If so, then:*

   > C: Vested remainder, subject to open, in fee

   > B: Nothing

   > If the court construes the language to allow A's children to graduate high school after turning 21, *then*:

   > B and C: Vested remainder, subject to open, in fee

   e. A has one child, B, who is 21 and has a GED.

   > The state of title is unclear; does a GED constitute "graduating high school," or is it a substitute for graduating high school? If the court strictly construes the grant, *then*:

   > A's children who reach 21: Contingent remainder in fee

   > If instead the court attempts to effectuate the grantor's intent, believes obtaining a GED satisfies the purpose of the condition, and/or interprets

the grant to further the policy of encouraging the successful completion of high school studies, *then*:

> B: Vested remainder, subject to open, in fee

13. O to A in fee tail, then to B in fee tail.

> B: Vested remainder in fee tail

14. O to A for life, then to B if B cares for A when A is infirm and over the age of 75 (A is younger than 75).

> B: Contingent remainder in fee simple absolute (unfulfilled condition precedent)

15. O to A for life, then to B if B marries C, otherwise to D (B has not yet married C).

> B: Contingent remainder in fee simple absolute (unfulfilled condition precedent).

> D: Alternative contingent remainder in fee simple absolute (unfulfilled condition precedent, which is the opposite of the condition B must meet—for D's remainder to vest, B must <u>not</u> marry C).

16. O to A for life.

> O has a reversion, not a remainder. Reversions are not classified as vested or contingent.

For problems 17–20, assume that your jurisdiction follows the common law rule of destructibility of contingent remainders. Determine whether the series of events causes any contingent remainders to be destroyed, and who owns the property once the events are completed.

17. O grants Blackacre to A for life, then if B has joined the military, to B in fee. Five years after the conveyance, A dies, and B has not yet joined the military (B is only 10 years old when A dies).

> O now owns Blackacre in fee. At the time of the conveyance, A owned a life estate, B owned a contingent remainder in fee, and O retained a reversion. When A dies, the contingency must be tested. Because B did not join the military, his contingent remainder did not vest and it is destroyed (it does not matter that B is too young to join the military; under the common law, a contingent remainder is always destroyed if it does not vest by the time the preceding estate expires—that may not seem "fair," but it is the law). O's reversion kicks in and O owns Blackacre in fee.

18. O grants Blackacre to A for life, then to B's children who reach age 21 for life, then to C. B has two children, D (who is 18) and E (who is 15). One month later, A conveys his entire interest in Blackacre to C.

> C now owns Blackacre in fee. At the time of the conveyance, A had a life estate, B's children who reach age 21 had a contingent remainder for life (the remainder was contingent since there were not any ascertained members of the class), and C had a vested remainder in fee. When A conveyed his entire interest to C, C obtained a life estate pur autre vie, which merged with C's vested remainder in fee, giving C a fee simple absolute. The contingent remainder belonging to B's children who reach age 21 was destroyed.

19. O grants Blackacre to A for life, then to B for life if B marries C, then to A in fee. At a later time, A conveys his entire interest in Blackacre to D.

   a. In addition, when A conveys his interests to D, B has not yet married C.

        D now owns Blackacre in fee. At the time of the grant, A had a life estate, B had a contingent remainder for life, and A had a vested remainder in fee. A's life estate and vested remainder in fee did not merge because they were given to A in the same grant. However, as soon as A conveyed both of them to D, the interests merged and B's contingent remainder was destroyed.

   b. In contrast to the prior example, B does marry C before A conveys his interests to D.

        When B married C, B's remainder vested. A vested remainder cannot be destroyed. Therefore, D's interests do not merge. The state of the title is as follows:

           D: Life estate pur autre vie for the life of A

           B: Vested remainder for life

           D: Vested remainder in fee

20. O grants Blackacre to A and the heirs of his body, then to B for life. At a later time, A conveys a life estate pur autre vie to O.

        At the time of the grant, A had a fee tail, B had a vested remainder for life, and O had a reversion. When A conveyed a life estate pur autre vie to O, O already had a reversion. However, these interests do not merge because B's remainder is vested and is not destroyed. A's grant did not disentail the fee tail, and A's bodily heirs will own the property when A dies.

For problems 21–24, identify the state of title. If events are described after the conveyance, give the state of title at each stage in the process (i.e., at the time of the conveyance, after the first event, and so on). Assume that the common law rule of destructibility applies.

21. T devises Blackacre to A for life, then to B for life if B becomes a pediatrician (T just died, and B is already a pediatrician).

        A: Life estate

        B: Vested remainder for life

        T's devisee/heir: Reversion

22. T devises Blackacre to A for life, then to T's children who reach age 20 (T, who just died, has three children, B, C, and D, but only B has reached 20). Tragically, all of T's children die in a car accident leaving T's funeral, and C and D were still not 20. A dies ten years later.

   At the time of the devise (i.e., T's death):

        A: Life estate

        B: Vested remainder, subject to open, in fee

   After the car accident:

        A: Life estate

        B's heirs/devisees: Vested remainder in fee

After A's death:

> B's heirs/devisees: Fee

23. O grants Blackacre to A for life, then to O's children if they all reach age 20 (O has three children, B, C, and D, but only B has reached age 20). A few years later, C turns 20. The day before D turns 20, B—a pilot—takes his siblings for a flight in his Cessna. B crashes just after takeoff and none of the siblings survive.

> *At the time of the grant:*
>
> > A: Life estate
> >
> > O's children: Contingent remainder in fee (all of O's children must reach 20 for the remainder to vest)
> >
> > O: Reversion
>
> *After C turns 20*: Nothing changes
>
> *After the plane crash:*
>
> > A: Life estate
> >
> > O: Reversion

24. O grants Blackacre to A in fee tail, then to B's children for the duration of B's life (B has no children). A dies three years later, leaving no issue besides his one daughter—C—behind. One year after A's death, B has a boy—D. Then, in another fifteen years, B dies, followed shortly thereafter by C's death (C has no issue).

> *At the time of the grant:*
>
> > A: Fee tail
> >
> > B's children: Contingent remainder in life estate pur autre vie (for the life of B) (contingent because B has no children)
> >
> > O: Reversion
>
> *At A's death:*
>
> > C: Fee tail
> >
> > B's children: Contingent remainder in life estate pur autre vie (for the life of B)
> >
> > O: Reversion
>
> *At D's birth:*
>
> > C: Fee tail
> >
> > D: Vested remainder, subject to open, in life estate pure autre vie (for the life of B)
> >
> > O: Reversion
>
> *At B's death:*
>
> > C: Fee tail
> >
> > O: Reversion
>
> *At C's death:*
>
> > O: Fee

CHAPTER 4

Answer problems 1–7.

1. When does the Rule in Shelley's Case apply?

   The Rule in Shelley's Case *only* applies when the grantor conveys a life interest to a grantee and, in the same grant, a *remainder* to that grantee's heirs.

2. What is the result of applying the Rule in Shelley's Case?

   After applying the Rule in Shelley's Case, the grantee owns the remainder granted to the grantee's heirs.

3. Does the Rule Against Perpetuities apply to all future interests?

   No. For example, the RAP cannot invalidate a future interest the grantor retained. Only three interests are threatened by the RAP. The two that we have learned so far are contingent and class remainders. The Rule is not literally opposed to *all* perpetuities, just some.

4. What is a life in being?

   A life in being is anyone alive at the time of the conveyance or at the death of the person devising the property. For our purposes, we generally focus on anyone named in the conveyance or will.

5. What is the time limitation of the RAP?

   21 years after the death of the lives in being; in other words, one generation after all generations alive at the time of the grant have died.

6. For an interest to be valid under the RAP, do we have to know that it will eventually vest within the applicable time limitation?

   No. We must know that it "will vest, *if at all*," within 21 years after the lives of all lives in being. In other words, we must know that the interest will *either* vest *or* cease to exist within 21 years after all lives in being have died.

7. When do you apply the RAP?

   You test whether the interests are valid under the RAP at the time of the grant or devise.

For problems 8–11, give the state of title on the face of the grant. If the Rule in Shelley's Case applies, give the state of title afterwards.

8. O conveys Blackacre to A for life, then to A's heirs in fee.

   Face of the grant:

      A: Life estate

      A's heirs: Contingent remainder in fee (A's heirs are not ascertainable until <u>after</u> A's death)

      O: Reversion

   By operation of the Rule in Shelley's Case:

      A: Life estate + vested remainder in fee = fee simple absolute

9. O conveys Blackacre to A for life, then to B for life, then to B's heirs.

    Face of the grant:

    A: Life estate

    B: Vested remainder in life estate

    B's heirs: Contingent remainder in fee simple absolute

    O: Reversion

    By operation of the Rule in Shelley's Case:

    A: Life estate

    B: Vested remainder in life estate + vested remainder in fee simple absolute = vested remainder in fee simple absolute

10. O conveys Blackacre to A for life, then to B for life, then to A's heirs.

    Face of the grant:

    A: Life estate

    B: Vested remainder in life estate

    A's heirs: Contingent remainder in fee

    O: Reversion

    By operation of the Rule in Shelley's Case:

    A: Life estate

    B: Vested remainder in life estate

    A: Vested remainder in fee simple absolute

    A's life estate and A's vested remainder in fee are separated by B's vested remainder; therefore, they do not merge.

11. O conveys Blackacre to A for life, then to all of A's children (A has no children).

    Face of the grant:

    A: Life estate

    A's children: Contingent remainder in fee simple absolute

    O: Reversion

    The Rule in Shelley's Case applies <u>only</u> to remainders in a grantee's "heirs," not to remainders to a grantee's children or issue.

For problems 12–23, first give the state of title on the face of the grant. Identify any interests that are threatened by the RAP. Test the interests, and give the state of title after applying the RAP. Apply the Rule in Shelley's Case and the Doctrine of Destructibility of Contingent Remainders as applicable.

<u>**Interests that are susceptible to the RAP are underlined.**</u>

12. O to A for life, then to B if humans walk on Mars.

    Face of the grant:

    A: Life estate

    B: <u>Contingent remainder in fee simple absolute</u> (condition precedent not yet met)

    O: Reversion

Under the destructibility rule, B's remainder must either vest or be destroyed by the expiration of the preceding estate, thus by A's death. A is the validating life, and the remainder is valid under the RAP.

13. O to A and the heirs of her body, then to B if B lives to be 75 (B is not yet 75).

Face of the grant:

A: Fee tail

B: <u>Contingent remainder in fee simple absolute</u> (condition precedent not yet met)

O: Reversion

The condition precedent will either be met, or not, during B's lifetime. B is thus a validating life, so his remainder is valid under the RAP.

14. O to A for life, then to A's children (A has one child, B).

Face of the grant:

A: Life estate

B: <u>Vested remainder, subject to open, in fee</u>

Because the remainder is to A's children, the class will close when A dies if A is a woman, or 9 months after A's death if A is a man. Regardless, the class will close at A's death due to the Rule of Convenience. A is therefore the validating life, and B's vested remainder, subject to open, in fee is valid.

15. O to A for life, then to the first person to walk on Mars.

Face of the grant:

A: Life estate

First person to walk on Mars: <u>Contingent remainder in fee simple absolute</u> (unascertained owner)

O: Reversion

Under the destructibility rule, the contingent remainder will either vest or be destroyed by the expiration of the preceding estate, thus by A's death. A is therefore the validating life, and the remainder is valid under the RAP.

16. O to A for life, then to B if B learns to play chess (B has never played chess).

Face of the grant:

A: Life estate

B: <u>Contingent remainder in fee simple absolute</u> (condition precedent not yet met)

O: Reversion

The condition precedent here—B learning to play chess—will be met, if at all, during B's lifetime. B is thus a validating life, and the interest is valid under the RAP. Moreover, under the destructibility rule, the remainder must either vest or be destroyed by A's death, making A an additional validating life (but remember, only one validating life is necessary for an interest to be valid under the RAP).

17. O to A in fee tail, then to B if B becomes a CEO (B is not yet a CEO).

> *Face of the grant*:
>
>> A: Fee tail
>>
>> B: <u>Contingent remainder in fee simple absolute</u> (condition precedent not yet met)
>>
>> O: Reversion

The condition precedent making the remainder contingent (B becoming a CEO) will clearly be met, if at all, during B's lifetime. B is a validating life, and his contingent remainder is valid.

18. O to A for life, then to A's children who reach 21 (A does not yet have any children).

> *Face of the grant*:
>
>> A: Life estate
>>
>> A's children who reach 21: <u>Contingent remainder in fee simple absolute</u> (unascertained owner)
>>
>> O: Reversion

Under the destructibility doctrine, the remainder must either vest or be destroyed by the expiration of the preceding estate (at A's death). A is therefore a validating life and the remainder is valid.

19. O to A for life, then to B if B's grandchildren graduate high school (none of B's grandchildren have yet graduated high school).

> *Face of the grant*:
>
>> A: Life estate
>>
>> B: <u>Contingent remainder in fee simple absolute</u> (condition precedent not yet met)
>>
>> O: Reversion

Under the destructibility doctrine, A is the validating life because the remainder must either vest or be destroyed by the expiration of the preceding estate (by A's death).

20. O to A in fee tail, then to B if Greece leaves the Eurozone.

> *Face of the grant*:
>
>> A: Fee tail
>>
>> B: <u>Contingent remainder in fee simple absolute</u> (condition precedent not yet met)
>>
>> O: Reversion

B's interest is void. Greece might leave the Eurozone more than 21 years after all lives in being (O, A, and B) have died. (Lives in being are only people; a country, like Greece, is not a "life" in being.) The destructibility doctrine does not save the remainder. A has a fee tail, which can pass indefinitely to A's issue, so the estate preceding B's might not expire until more than 21 years have passed since the death of the last life in being (unlike a life estate, it is not guaranteed to expire at A's death).

> *The state of title after applying the RAP is*:
>
>> A: Fee tail

O: Reversion

21. O to A for life, then to A's youngest grandchild then living for life, then to O's oldest child then living for life, then, if any of A's other grandchildren are still alive, to those grandchildren.

Face of the grant:

A: Life estate

A's youngest grandchild then living: <u>Contingent remainder in life estate</u>

O's oldest child then living: <u>Contingent remainder in life estate</u>

A's grandchildren who are still alive: <u>Contingent remainder in fee</u>

O: Reversion

The first contingent remainder is valid because, by the express terms of the grant, A's youngest grandchild <u>then living</u> will be ascertained at A's death. A is the validating life also because the remainder must vest by A's death due to the doctrine of destructibility. The second contingent remainder is invalid because there is no validating life. A's youngest grandchild is not a validating life because A's youngest grandchild might not be a life in being and might not die for more than 21 years after all lives in being (here, the only known ones are O and A) have died. The contingent remainder in A's grandchildren still alive is also void for the same reason. *Thus*:

A: Life estate

A's youngest grandchild then living: Contingent remainder in life estate

O: Reversion

22. T devises Blackacre to A, his child with a disability, for life, then for life to the last person who cares for A for more than 15 years, then to T's oldest descendant then living.

Face of the devise:

A: Life estate

The last person to care for A for more than 15 years: <u>Contingent remainder in life estate</u> (unascertained owner)

T's oldest descendant then living: <u>Contingent remainder in fee</u> (unascertained owner)

T's devisee/heir: Reversion

Because the last person to care for A for more than 15 years will be known at A's death, A is a validating life for the first contingent remainder. A is also the validating life for this contingent remainder because of destructibility.

However, because the last person to care for A for more than 15 years may not be born at the time of the grant, and we will not know who T's oldest descendant alive at the caretaker's death is until the caretaker dies, the second contingent remainder is not tied to any particular life in being and is invalid; this second contingent remainder might exist without vesting for more than 21 years after all lives in being (here A is the only known one) die. The fact that this is a devise does not change the result because at T's death (when the transfer becomes effective) we still will not know who the oldest living descendant will be at the time of the unknown caregiver's death; T might have more descendants born after T's death.

After applying the RAP:

> A: Life estate

> The last person to care for A for more than 15 years:
> Contingent remainder in life estate

> T's devisee/heir: Reversion

Because the invalid remainder was created by T's will, you may wonder how T's devisee could own an interest under the will after the RAP is applied. Wills often have residuary clauses that specify a devisee for any other property the testator owns (e.g., "I devise all of my other property, both real and personal, not specified above, to Z"). If T's will contained a residuary clause, then the clause implicitly designated who now owns T's *reversion*, and the RAP does not apply to reversions. If there is no such clause in T's will, then there is partial intestacy (i.e., T's will did not cover all his property), and the interest would pass to T's heir.

23. T executes a will devising Blackacre to A for life, then to B for life, then for life sequentially to each of A's children alive at T's death, beginning with the eldest, then for life to the next eldest until all A's children alive at T's death have owned Blackacre, then to the eldest then living descendant of A in fee. At the time, A has no children. Ten years later, T dies. He never sold Blackacre or changed his will, and A has two children, C and D (C is older than D).

This question tests whether you pay close attention to the timing of testing the RAP. The interests are created by the will when T dies, not when the will is executed. You therefore apply that RAP at the time of T's death, not at the time the will is written:

Face of the devise (when T dies):

> A: Life estate

> B: Vested remainder in life estate

> C: Vested remainder in life estate

> D: Vested remainder in life estate

> A's eldest then living descendant: <u>Contingent remainder in fee</u> (unascertained owner)

> T's devisee/heir: Reversion

Because the devise is not effective until T's death, "for life sequentially to each of A's children alive at T's death" does not create contingent remainders, because we know who the owners are at T's death when the devises become effective. Thus, the only remainder that is contingent is the one to A's eldest then living descendant, a person who can't be ascertained until the expiration of the last preceding estate. But, because we know C and D are lives in being at the time of T's death, A, B, C, and D together are the measuring lives, and the contingent remainder will both vest and become possessory, if at all, on the death of the last of them. The contingent remainder therefore stands.

A likely mistake when analyzing this problem is to describe the interests at the time of the writing of the will (in other words, to treat it like a grant at the time of the writing), rather than when T dies. This would lead you to mistakenly conclude that the remainder that eventually vests in C and D would be contingent at the time of the writing, and you would then likely further mistakenly conclude that the remainders to D and to A's eldest then living descendant are invalid because C and D were not lives in being at the time of the writing.

Problems 24 and 25 explore two legal concept that flow from the RAP. Remember, the RAP is concerned with what is theoretically possible, not with what is most probable. Give the state of title.

24. O conveys Blackacre to A in fee tail, then to A's last child to reach age 30 (A is 80 and she has two children, ages 50 and 40).

     Face of the grant:

     A: Fee tail

     A's last child to reach age 30: <u>Contingent remainder in fee simple absolute</u> (unascertained owner—see below)

     O: Reversion

     Although A is 80, the law assumes that she can have another child. This is the concept (more accurately, fiction) of the ***fertile octogenarian*** (which you might accurately note seems inconsistent with the common law's insistence otherwise of presuming normal biological reproduction). We therefore do not assume that the current youngest child (the 40 year old) will necessarily be the last child of A to reach 30. (Of course, the grant does not say "natural child," so in addition to the assumption of unusual fertility, it is possible that A could adopt a child.) Because the owner is unascertained, the remainder is contingent and must be tested by the RAP. The destructibility rule does not save the remainder because the preceding estate is a fee tail and thus is not certain to expire during a life in being (specifically, at A's death). If A has another child, this child might not reach age 30 for more than 21 years after the death of every life in being (in this case, O, A, and A's two children). There is no validating life, and the remainder is void under the RAP.

     State of title after the RAP:

     A: Fee tail

     O: Reversion

25. O conveys Blackacre to A for life, then to A's widow for life, then to A's children alive at A's widow's death.

     Face of the grant:

     A: Life estate

     A's widow: <u>Contingent remainder in life estate</u> (unascertained owner)

     A's children alive at A's widow's death: <u>Contingent remainder in fee simple absolute</u> (unascertained owner)

     O: Reversion (following the contingent remainder)

     We have two contingent remainders, both of which must be tested by the RAP.

     First, the remainder to A's widow is contingent only because we do not know who A's widow is. However, if A has a widow, we will know who she is at his death, and if he doesn't have a widow, then this interest will never vest because there will never be an owner, and thus the remainder will cease to exist. A therefore is the validating life for his widow's contingent remainder, which is valid.

Second, the contingent remainder to A's children alive at A's widow's death will only vest, if at all, after both preceding interests have expired (i.e., after A and his widow have both died). Because A's widow could outlive A by more than 21 years, A cannot be the validating life for this second remainder. The widow cannot be a validating life because ***we do not know if she is a life in being.*** We have no idea who will be A's widow (if at all) when he dies, and in fact, she may be someone who is not yet born. Because it is not certain that the second remainder will vest, if at all, within 21 years of a life in being, the second remainder is invalid, due to the phenomenon of the ***potential unborn widow***.

State of title after the RAP:

A: Life estate

A's widow: Contingent remainder in life estate

O: Reversion

CHAPTER 5

For problems 1–5, identify the attributes of property ownership associated with each interest.

1. Fee simple determinable

   Alienable, devisable, and inheritable

2. Fee subject to a condition subsequent

   Alienable, devisable, and inheritable

3. Life estate determinable

   Only alienable for the owner's lifetime; neither inheritable nor devisable (except for a life estate pur autre vie).

4. Possibility of reverter

   Common law: Inheritable, but not alienable or devisable

   Modern law: Alienable, devisable, and inheritable

5. Right of entry

   Common law: Inheritable, but not alienable or devisable

   Modern law: Alienable, devisable, and inheritable

Answer problems 6–9.

6. Compare and contrast a determinable estate and an estate subject to a condition subsequent.

   The defeasance clause of a determinable estate is introduced with temporal language, while the defeasance clause for an estate subject to a condition subsequent is introduced with conditional language. The defeasance clause is directly attached to a determinable estate, but punctuation separates the defeasance clause from an estate subject to a condition subsequent. Finally, a determinable estate ends automatically when the condition is violated, but an estate subject to a condition subsequent requires the grantor to enter and reclaim the property to terminate the estate.

7. Compare and contrast a possibility of reverter and a right of entry.

    A possibility of reverter follows a determinable estate, but a right of entry follows an estate subject to a condition subsequent. The possibility of reverter entitles the grantor to have title automatically revert back when the condition is violated, but a right of entry requires the grantor to enter and reclaim the property after the condition is violated.

8. What are the differences between a condition subsequent and a condition precedent?

    A condition precedent introduces or is connected to a remainder, making it contingent, and the contingent remainder does not cut off a property interest since it always waits patiently. In contrast, a condition subsequent can cut an estate short. Moreover, a condition precedent is either directly attached to or before the interest it modifies. On the other hand, a condition subsequent is never directly attached to the interest it modifies (it is separated by punctuation and it follows the interest that it can cut short).

9. What are the differences between a reversion and a possibility of reverter or a right of entry?

    A reversion follows a contingent remainder or an expirable estate, and in the latter case, it waits patiently until the previous estate expires naturally. In contrast, a possibility of reverter or a right of entry follows a defeasible estate and can cut that estate short.

For problems 10–11, identify who owns the property once every event has occurred.

10. O conveys Blackacre to Caleb as long as chickens are raised on Blackacre. Caleb immediately starts raising chickens. When Caleb subsequently realizes that he could make more money by growing watermelons on the property, he butchers his chickens and plants melons.

    Caleb owns a fee simple determinable, and O has retained a possibility of reverter. As soon as Caleb stops raising chickens, his estate is cut short and the title reverts back to O in fee.

11. O grants Blackacre to Christopher, but if Christopher stops taking piano lessons, then O retains the right to reenter and claim the property. At the time of the grant, Christopher is regularly taking piano lessons. After a few years—when he begins college—Christopher cancels his lessons. O never learns that Christopher has stopped taking lessons, and O never returns to Blackacre.

    Christopher owns a fee subject to a condition subsequent, and O has retained a right of entry. Although Christopher violated the condition, Christopher retains ownership because O has not reentered and reclaimed Christopher's estate in land.

Provide the state of title for the conveyances in problems 12–21.

12. O to A for life as long as A regularly attends church.

    A: Life estate determinable

    O: Possibility of reverter (for the life of A)

    O: Reversion

13. O to A, but if A stops attending church, then O may reenter and claim the land.

    A: Fee simple subject to a condition subsequent

    O: Right of entry

14. O to A until a man walks on Mars.

> A: Fee simple determinable
>
> O: Possibility of reverter

15. O to A during the reign of Queen Elizabeth II.

> A: Fee simple determinable
>
> O: Possibility of reverter

16. O to A, but if Queen Elizabeth ceases to reign, then to O.

> A: Fee simple subject to a condition subsequent
>
> O: Right of entry

17. O to A for life, but if the Republicans gain a supermajority in both houses of Congress while a Republican is also president, then to O.

> A: Life estate subject to a condition subsequent
>
> O: Right of entry (in life estate pur autre vie for the life of A)
>
> O: Reversion

18. O to A and his heirs, but if A or one of A's bodily heirs attends State University, then O may enter and reclaim the property.

> A: Fee simple subject to a condition subsequent
>
> O: Right of entry

19. O to A and his heirs as long as a natural gas well is operated on the property.

> A: Fee simple determinable
>
> O: Possibility of reverter

20. O to A for life while A farms the property.

> A: Life estate determinable
>
> O: Possibility of reverter (in life estate pur autre vie for the life of A)
>
> O: Reversion

21. O to A in fee tail, then to O's last child to graduate high school in fee tail, then to O's children who reach 20 and are employed by that age, otherwise to B and his heirs as long as the land is farmed (O does not yet have any children).

> *Face of the grant*:
>
> A: Fee tail
>
> O's last child to graduate high school: <u>Contingent remainder in fee tail</u>
>
> O's children who reach 20 and are employed by that age: <u>Contingent remainder in fee</u>
>
> B: <u>Alternative contingent remainder in fee simple determinable</u>
>
> O: Possibility of reverter
>
> O: Reversion (because of destructibility)

Do the contingent remainders survive the RAP? The contingent remainder in fee tail is invalid. Such a child of O is clearly not a life in being because O has no children. One of O's children might graduate high school more than 21 years after the death of the last life in being (O, A, or B). Destructibility does not save the interest because the preceding interest (A's interest) is in fee tail and might continue indefinitely and thus not expire within the required time period.

However, the contingent remainder to O's children who reach 20 and are employed by that age is valid. O is the validating life; the remainder will vest or fail within 21 years of O's death (remember, we assume natural reproduction). B's alternative contingent remainder is valid for the same reason.

After the RAP:

> A: Fee tail
>
> O's children who reach 20 and are employed by that age: Contingent remainder in fee
>
> B: Alternative contingent remainder in fee simple determinable
>
> O: Possibility of reverter
>
> O: Reversion

Problem 22 contains a pair of conveyances and a series of subsequent factual developments. For both grants, analyze the state of the title at the time of the grant and then at each point in the chronological chain. Assume there are no statutes of limitations.

22. O grants Greenacre to A as long as it is used for residential purposes.

O grants Greenacre to A, but if Greenacre is used for other than residential purposes, O may enter and reclaim.

a. A moves into the house on the day of the grant.

A: Fee simple determinable

O: Possibility of reverter

A: Fee simple subject to a condition subsequent

O: Right of entry

b. Four years later A starts a computer repair business in his basement while continuing to live in the house.

A: Fee simple determinable

O: Possibility of reverter

A: Fee simple subject to a condition subsequent (condition violated).

O: Right of entry

A still uses the lot for residential purposes, i.e., he lives there, so the defeasance clause has not been violated; it does not say "only" for residential purposes.

This condition prohibits any non-residential use; therefore, even though A still lives there, he is using the house to run a business and triggers the condition. However, because O has a right of entry, he must make an affirmative action to reclaim the property, and the condition does not automatically transfer title.

c.   One month after A opens his business, O tries to kick A out of the house.

A: Fee simple determinable	O: Fee simple absolute
O: Possibility of reverter	O has now taken the steps necessary to assert his right of entry, and because the condition was violated, he now owns a fee.
Because A has not violated the condition, O has no grounds to eject A, and his attempt will fail.	

Assume that your jurisdiction has a 30-year statute of limitations for possibilities of reverter and rights of entry. Moreover, assume that a right of entry must be exercised within two years of when the condition was violated. Give the state of title after each event in problems 23–24.

23. O conveys Blackacre to A in 2015. The conveyance states, *"O to A for life as long as A farms the property."* Because of health problems, A stops farming in 2040. O attempts to enter and reclaim Blackacre in 2043.

> *Face of the grant*:
>
> > A: Life estate determinable
> >
> > O: Possibility of reverter (in life estate pur autre vie for the life of A)
> >
> > O: Reversion
>
> *When A stops farming in 2040*:
>
> > O: Fee (life estate pur autre vie + reversion = fee)

Because O's possibility of reverter operated as a matter of law, it is unnecessary for him to enter and reclaim Blackacre. O owns the fee in 2040. The possibility of reverter was still valid because it had not yet existed for 30 years.

24. O conveys Whiteacre to A in 2020: *"O to A, but if A ever uses Whiteacre for commercial purposes, then O may enter and reclaim the property."* In 2030, A opens a garden nursery on Whiteacre; three years later, O claims title to the property.

> *Face of the grant*:
>
> > A: Fee simple subject to a condition subsequent
> >
> > O: Right of entry
>
> *When A opens the garden nursery in 2030*:
>
> > A: Fee simple subject to a condition subsequent
> >
> > O: Right of entry
>
> *When O tries to claim title*:
>
> > A: Fee simple absolute. The statute of limitations requires O to exercise the right of entry within two years of a violation of the condition. Because O waited three years, O lost all rights to Whiteacre.

CHAPTER 6

Answer problems 1–8.

1. A conveyance creates a defeasible fee; the condition is introduced by words of temporal limitation, and the condition is directly attached to the estate. The future interest is in the grantor. What is the present estate, and what is the future interest following it?

    > Fee simple determinable

    > Possibility of reverter

2. A conveyance creates a defeasible fee; the condition is introduced by conditional language, and punctuation separates the defeasible estate from the conditional language. The future interest is in the grantor. What is the present estate, and what is the future interest following it?

    > Fee subject to a condition subsequent

    > Right of entry

3. A conveyance creates a defeasible fee; the condition is introduced by words of temporal limitation, and the condition is directly attached to the estate. The future interest is in a grantee. What is the present estate, and what is the future interest following it?

    > Fee simple determinable

    > Executory interest

4. A conveyance creates a defeasible fee; the condition is introduced by conditional language, and punctuation separates the defeasible estate from the conditional language. The future interest is in a grantee. What is the present estate, and what is the future interest following it?

    > Fee subject to an executory limitation

    > Executory interest

5. What are the differences between a fee subject to a condition subsequent and a fee subject to an executory limitation?

    > A fee subject to a condition subsequent is followed by an interest in the grantor (a right of entry), whereas a fee subject to an executory limitation is followed by an interest in a grantee (an executory interest). A fee subject to a condition subsequent does not automatically end at violation; the grantor must enter and reclaim the property. By contrast, a fee subject to an executory limitation ends as soon as the condition is violated.

6. What is the difference between a shifting and a springing executory interest?

    > A shifting executory interest follows and cuts off an interest conveyed in the original grant to a grantee (it shifts from one grantee to another); a springing executory interest follows and cuts off an interest retained in the original grant by the grantor (it springs from the grantor to a grantee).

7. To what interests does the Doctrine of Worthier Title apply?

    > Any future interest in the grantor's heirs

8. How do you distinguish the Doctrine of Worthier Title from the Rule in Shelley's Case?

> The Doctrine of Worthier Title applies to *any* interest in the *grantor's* heirs, whereas the Rule in Shelley's Case applies to a *remainder* in a *grantee's* heirs where the grantee is conveyed a life interest in the same grant.

For problems 9–13, identify whether the executory interest is shifting or springing.

9. O grants Blackacre to A as long as A never fails to submit his federal tax return, then to B.

> Shifting

10. O grants Blackacre to A when A balances his budget.

> Springing

11. O grants Blackacre to A, but if A incurs more than $5,000 in debt, then to B.

> Shifting

12. O grants Blackacre to A for life, then to B six months after A's death.

> Springing

13. T devises Blackacre to A when A becomes a grandfather.

> Springing

For problems 14–17, identify the defeasible fee that A owns as well as the future interest following it.

14. O grants Blackacre to A as long as the property is farmed, then to B.

> A: Fee simple determinable
>
> B: Shifting executory interest in fee

15. O grants Blackacre to A, but if A ever joins the Navy, then O may enter and reclaim.

> A: Fee subject to a condition subsequent
>
> O: Right of entry

16. O grants Blackacre to A until A becomes a Marine.

> A: Fee simple determinable
>
> O: Possibility of reverter

17. T devises Blackacre to A, but if A runs for political office, then to B.

> A: Fee subject to an executory limitation
>
> B: Shifting executory interest in fee

For problems 18–20, identify the defeasible life estate that A owns as well as the future interest(s) following it.

18. T devises Blackacre to A for life, but if A opens a bar on Blackacre, then to B.

> A: Life estate subject to an executory limitation
>
> B: Shifting executory interest in fee
>
> T's heirs/devisees: Reversion

19. O grants Blackacre to A for life as long as A remains a Libertarian, then to B.

> A: Life estate determinable
>
> B: Shifting executory interest in life estate pur autre vie (for the life of A)
>
> B: Vested remainder in fee

20. O grants Blackacre to A for life, but if B quits smoking, then to B.

> A: Life estate subject to an executory limitation
>
> B: Shifting executory interest in fee
>
> O: Reversion

Provide the state of title on the face of the grant for problems 21–31. If the Doctrine of Worthier Title or the Rule in Shelley's Case applies, also provide the state of title after applying the rule(s).

21. O to A for life, then to O's heirs.

> *Face of the grant*:
>
> > A: Life estate
> >
> > O's heirs: Contingent remainder in fee
> >
> > O: Reversion
>
> *After applying the Doctrine of Worthier Title*:
>
> > A: Life estate
> >
> > O: Reversion

22. O to A, but if A ever starts smoking, then to O's heirs.

> *Face of the grant*:
>
> > A: Fee subject to an executory limitation
> >
> > O's heirs: Shifting executory interest in fee
>
> *After applying the Doctrine of Worthier Title*:
>
> > A: Fee subject to a condition subsequent
> >
> > O: Right of entry

23. O to A as long as the land is farmed, then to A's heirs.

> A: Fee simple determinable
>
> A's heirs: Shifting executory interest in fee
>
> The Rule in Shelley's Case only applies to remainders.

24. O to A for life, then to O's children (O has no children).

> A: Life estate
>
> O's children: Contingent remainder in fee
>
> O: Reversion
>
> The Doctrine of Worthier Title only applies to future interests in the grantor's <u>heirs</u>.

25. O to A for life, then to B for life, then to A's heirs.

    Face of the grant:

        A: Life estate

        B: Vested remainder in life estate

        A's heirs: Contingent remainder in fee

        O: Reversion

    After applying the Rule in Shelley's Case:

        A: Life estate

        B: Vested remainder in life estate

        A: Vested remainder in fee

26. O to A as long as the land is farmed, then to O's heirs.

    Face of the grant:

        A: Fee simple determinable

        O's heirs: Shifting executory interest in fee

    After applying the Doctrine of Worthier Title:

        A: Fee simple determinable

        O: Possibility of reverter

27. O to A for life until A starts raising chickens, then at A's death to B.

    A: Life estate determinable

    O: Possibility of reverter in life estate pur autre vie

    B: Vested remainder in fee

28. O to A for life, but if A is ever elected to political office, then to B for the life of A.

    A: Life estate subject to an executory limitation

    B: Shifting executory interest in life estate pur autre vie

    O: Reversion

29. O to A until A no longer makes maple syrup on the property.

    A: Fee simple determinable

    O: Possibility of reverter

30. O to A when A's first child is born (A has no children).

    O: Fee subject to an executory limitation (because "when" is temporal, some courts might consider this to be a fee simple determinable)

    A: Springing executory interest in fee

31. O to A, but if A stops farming the property or B graduates law school, then to B.

    A: Fee subject to an executory limitation

    B: Shifting executory interest in fee

    Note: There are two ways the condition may be violated (A could stop farming, or B could graduate from law school), and either one will cause B to own the property.

CHAPTER 7

Answer problems 1–4.

1. When a remainder is subject to a condition, how can you determine whether the remainder is contingent or vested?

    If the condition is a condition precedent, then it is a contingent remainder. If the condition is a condition subsequent, then it is a vested remainder. A condition precedent either precedes the remainder or is grammatically attached to it, while a condition subsequent follows the remainder and is set off from it by punctuation.

2. When is a vested remainder in an estate subject to an executory limitation?

    If the executory interest can only cut off the vested remainder after it becomes a present estate (and thus is no longer a remainder), then the vested remainder is in an estate subject to an executory limitation.

3. When is a vested remainder subject to divestment?

    If the executory interest can only cut off the vested remainder *before* it becomes a present estate (and thus is still a remainder), then the vested remainder is subject to divestment.

4. When is a vested remainder both subject to divestment and in an estate subject to an executory limitation?

    If the executory interest can cut off the vested remainder both before *and* after it becomes a present estate, then the vested remainder is subject to divestment and in an estate subject to an executory limitation.

For problems 5–11, identify whether the vested remainder to B is subject to divestment, in an estate subject to an executory limitation, or both.

5. T devises Blackacre to A for life, then to B, but if B failed to visit T before his death, then to C.

    Subject to divestment

6. O grants Blackacre to A for life, then to B, but if B ever stops providing for A's family after A's death, then to C.

    In an estate subject to an executory limitation

7. O grants Blackacre to A for life, then to B, but if C publishes a book on Estates in Land and Future Interests, then to C.

    Both

8. O grants Blackacre to A for life, then to B, but if B digs a new well on the premises, then to C.

    In an estate subject to an executory limitation

9. O grants Blackacre to A for life, then to B, but if A or B renovates the house on Blackacre, then to C.

    Both

10. T devises Blackacre to A for life, then to B, but if T's youngest child retires after A's death, then to that child.

    In an estate subject to an executory limitation

11. O grants Blackacre to A for life, then to B, but if A ever leaves the law firm O founded, then to C.

> Subject to divestment

For problems 12–17, determine whether B's interest is a contingent remainder or a vested remainder subject to divestment and/or in an estate subject to an executory limitation.

12. O grants Blackacre to A for life, then to B if B has learned to play the guitar.

> Contingent remainder in fee

13. O grants Blackacre to A for life, then to B, but if B has not yet learned to play the guitar, then to C.

> Vested remainder, subject to divestment, in fee

14. O grants Blackacre to A for life, then to A's children (A has one child, B).

> Vested remainder, subject to open, in fee

15. O grants Blackacre to A for life, then to A's son B, but if A has more children before his death, then to all of A's children (A has one child, B).

> Vested remainder, subject to divestment, in fee

16. O grants Blackacre to A for life, then to O's only son B, but if O has more children, then to all of O's children.

> Vested remainder, subject to divestment, in fee subject to an executory limitation.

17. O grants Blackacre to A for life, then if A does not have any sons, to O's son B (A has no children).

> Contingent remainder in fee

For problems 18–21, identify every interest that is subject to divestment and/or in an estate subject to an executory limitation.

18. O grants Blackacre to A for life, then to B, but if B ever leaves the law firm O founded, then at that time to C.

> A's life estate is subject to an executory limitation.

> B's vested remainder in fee is subject to divestment and subject to an executory limitation.

19. O grants Blackacre to A for life, then to B, but if B ever raises chickens on Blackacre, then to C.

> B's vested remainder is in fee subject to an executory limitation.

20. O grants Blackacre to A for life, then to B, but if A voluntarily retires, then at that time to A's son C.

> A's life estate is subject to an executory limitation.

> B's vested remainder is subject to divestment in fee.

21. T devises Blackacre to A for life, then to B, but if T dies childless, then to T's brother C.

> B's vested remainder is subject to divestment in fee.

Putting it together: for problems 22 and 23, give the state of title.

22. O conveys Blackacre to A for life, then to B for life, but if C outlives A, then to C.

> A: Life estate
>
> B: Vested remainder, subject to divestment, in a life estate
>
> C: Shifting executory interest in fee
>
> O: Reversion
>
> An executory limitation is presumed to apply only to the immediately preceding estate, unless specifically stated otherwise. A's life estate is therefore not subject to the executory limitation. B's remainder is subject to divestment because the condition subsequent will be tested right at A's death and thus can only keep B's interest from becoming possessory—it will not apply to B's interest after it becomes a present estate.

23. O conveys Blackacre to A for life, then to B for life unless B becomes a pilot, then to C, but if C becomes a pilot, then to D.

> A: Life estate
>
> B: <u>Contingent remainder in life estate</u>
>
> C: Vested remainder, subject to divestment, in fee subject to an executory limitation
>
> D: Shifting executory interest in fee
>
> B's interest does not violate the RAP because B is a validating life. A is also a validating life because of destructibility. C's remainder is vested, subject to divestment, and subject to an executory limitation because the condition subsequent to it could affect C's interest either before or after it becomes possessory.

CHAPTER 8

Answer problem 1.

1. To what interests does the RAP apply?

> Contingent remainders, class remainders, and executory interests

Provide the state of title on the face of the grant for problems 2–7. Test any executory interests under the RAP, and then provide the state of title after applying the RAP.

2. O to A until any of O's children reach 18, then to B.

> *Face of the grant*:
>
> > A: Fee simple determinable
> >
> > B: <u>Shifting executory interest in fee</u>
>
> The executory interest is valid under the RAP because any child of O would reach 18 less than 21 years after O's death, making O the validating life.

3. O to A, but if A's heir or devisee opens a restaurant on the premises, then to B.

> *Face of the grant*:
>
> > A: Fee simple subject to an executory limitation
> >
> > B: <u>Shifting executory interest in fee</u>

We will know who A's heir or devisee is at A's death; however, that person may be unborn at the time of the grant and could violate the condition more than 21 years after O, A, and B have died. There is no validating life and the interest is void.

After the RAP:

A: Fee simple absolute

4. T devises Blackacre to A, but if T's children ever become destitute, then to those children.

Face of the devise:

A: Fee simple subject to an executory limitation

T's children relying on food stamps: <u>Shifting executory interest in fee</u>

Because T devised the property, when this interest was created (at T's death), any children of T must be born (or in their mother's womb, if T is a man), and thus T's children are lives in being. Their executory interest is valid under the RAP.

5. O to A as long as any of O's children are alive and not older than 21, then to B (O has one child, C, who is 9).

Face of the grant:

A: Fee simple determinable

B: <u>Shifting executory interest in fee</u>

O's children may not yet all be alive and thus not all lives in being. O cannot be a validating life because the last of O's children to be born might not be "older than 21" until more than 21 years after O dies (though perhaps O's child may reach 21 if O is a woman and O dies the day her child is born). A and B cannot be validating lives because O's last child could be born after their death, and thus that child could become older than 21 more than 21 years after A and B die.

After the RAP:

A: Fee simple determinable

O: Possibility of reverter

6. O to A, but if chickens are ever raised on the property, then O may enter and reclaim the property.

Face of the grant:

A: Fee subject to a condition subsequent

O: Right of entry

The RAP does not apply to rights of entry.

7. O to A, but if any of O's children ever go on a mission trip to the Philippines, then to those children.

Face of the grant:

A: Fee subject to an executory limitation

O's children who go on a mission trip to the Philippines: <u>Shifting executory interest in fee</u>

O's children may not yet all be alive and thus not all lives in being. It is possible that an unborn child of O could go on such a mission trip more than 21 years after O and A have died.

After the RAP:

A: Fee simple absolute

For problems 8–10, provide the state of title at the time of the grant and after each stated event. Assume contingent remainders are not destructible.

8. O conveys Blackacre to A for life, then one year later to B. Several years after the conveyance, A dies.

   Face of the grant:

   A: Life estate

   O: Reversion (in fee subject to an executory limitation)

   B: <u>Springing executory interest in fee</u>

   B's interest is valid under the RAP because the executory interest will become possessory one year after A dies, making A the validating life. The state of the title on the face of the grant thus stands at the time of the grant.

   After A's death:

   O: Fee subject to an executory limitation

   B: Springing executory interest in fee

9. O conveys Blackacre to A for life, then to B if B ever attends Harvard. Years later, when A dies, B still has not attended Harvard. However, two years after A's death, B attends Harvard.

   Face of the grant:

   A: Life estate

   B: <u>Contingent remainder in fee</u>

   O: Reversion

   B's contingent remainder is valid because the condition—B attending Harvard—is tied to B's life, making him the validating life. The state of the title on the face of the grant thus stands at the time of the grant.

   After A's death:

   O: Fee simple subject to an executory limitation

   B: Springing executory interest in fee

   When B attends Harvard:

   B: Fee simple absolute

10. O conveys Blackacre to A for life, then to B for life if B outlives O, then to C two years after either A's, B's, or O's death (whichever comes latest). Five years after the conveyance, B dies. Two years later, O dies. Finally, A dies.

    Face of the grant:

    A: Life estate

    B: <u>Contingent remainder in life estate</u>

    O: Reversion (in fee subject to an executory limitation)

C: <u>Springing executory interest in fee</u>

B's remainder is valid because it will either vest or cease to exist when B dies, or when O dies (if O dies first). C's executory interest is valid because it expressly becomes possessory two years after the last of the three mentioned lives in being dies, which is thus less than 21 years after the lives of all lives in being. The state of the title on the face of the grant thus stands at the time of the grant.

After B's death:

A: Life estate

O: Reversion (in fee subject to an executory limitation)

C: Springing executory interest in fee

After O's death:

A: Life estate

O's heir/devisee: Reversion (in fee subject to an executory limitation)

C: Springing executory interest in fee

After A's death:

O's heir/devisee: Fee simple subject to an executory limitation

C: Springing executory interest in fee

Putting it together: Provide the state of title (both before and after the RAP) for the conveyances in problems 11–18. Assume that the Rule in Shelley's Case and the Doctrine of Worthier Title apply. If it makes a difference whether contingent remainders are destructible, then provide both answers.

11. O to A for life, then to B, but if anyone ever builds a factory on the premises, then to C.

Face of the grant:

A: Life estate

B: Vested remainder, subject to divestment, in fee subject to an executory limitation

C: <u>Shifting executory interest in fee</u>

The condition subsequent to B's remainder is potentially perpetual, making it and the executory interest void.

After the RAP:

A: Life estate

B: Vested remainder in fee

12. O to A in fee tail, then to B as long as corn is grown on the property, then to C.

Face of the grant:

A: Fee tail

B: Vested remainder in fee simple determinable

C: <u>Shifting executory interest in fee</u>

The defeasance clause on B's vested remainder and upon which C's executory interest depends is potentially perpetual, making C's interest invalid.

After the RAP:

     A: Fee tail

     B: Vested remainder in fee simple determinable

     O: Possibility of reverter

13. T devises Blackacre to A for life, then to T's children, but if any of T's grandchildren climb Mt. Everest, then to the first grandchild to do so (T has two children at her death).

     Face of the devise:

         A: Life estate

         T's children: Vested remainder, subject to divestment, in fee subject to an executory limitation

         T's first grandchild to climb Mt. Everest: <u>Shifting executory interest in fee</u>

The grandchild's executory interest is void. This is a will and thus any children T has will be born when the will takes effect (at T's death). However, T could have more grandchildren born after his death, and an unborn grandchild could first climb Mt. Everest more than 21 years after all lives in being have died.

After the RAP:

     A: Life estate

     T's children: Vested remainder in fee

14. O to A, but if a person ever walks on Mars, then to B.

     Face of the grant:

         A: Fee subject to an executory limitation

         B: <u>Shifting executory interest in fee</u>

Because this condition is potentially perpetual, we must strike the condition and the executory interest.

After the RAP:

     A: Fee

15. O to A for life, then to B if a person walks on Mars.

     Face of the grant:

         A: Life estate

         B: <u>Contingent remainder in fee</u>

         O: Reversion

After the RAP:

If contingent remainders are destructible, then B's remainder must vest by the expiration of the preceding estate (by A's death) or be destroyed. A is therefore the validating life and B's interest is valid.

If contingent remainders are not destructible, then B's interest is invalid, because a person could walk on Mars at some point in the indefinite future more than 21 years after all lives in being (here, O, A, and B) have died.

This leaves:

> A: Life estate
>
> O: Reversion

16. O to A as long as the house on the premises remains standing, then to B.

> *Face of the grant*:
>
> > A: Fee simple determinable
> >
> > B: <u>Shifting executory interest in fee</u>
>
> The defeasance clause on A's fee simple determinable and upon which B's executory interest depends is potentially perpetual, making B's interest invalid.
>
> *After the RAP*:
>
> > A: Fee simple determinable
> >
> > O: Possibility of reverter

17. T devises Blackacre to A, but if any of T's children survive A, then to those children.

> *Face of the devise*:
>
> > A: Fee simple subject to an executory limitation
> >
> > T's children who survive A: <u>Shifting executory interest in fee</u>
>
> The interest is valid. We will know whether any of T's children survive A when A dies, making A the validating life.

18. O to A for life, then to B for life, then to B's youngest child for life, then if B's youngest child's heirs are adults, to that child's heirs.

> *Face of the grant*:
>
> > A: Life estate
> >
> > B: Vested remainder in life estate
> >
> > B's youngest child: <u>Contingent remainder in life estate</u> (unascertained owner)
> >
> > B's youngest child's heirs: <u>Contingent remainder in fee</u> (unascertained owner and condition not met)
> >
> > O: Reversion
>
> Because an expirable interest was conveyed to B's youngest child, and in the same grant a remainder was conveyed to that child's heirs, the Rule in Shelley's Case applies. *The state of the title after applying the Rule in Shelley's Case is*:
>
> > A: Life estate
> >
> > B: Vested remainder in life estate
> >
> > B's youngest child: <u>Contingent remainder in life estate</u> (unascertained owner)
> >
> > B's youngest child: <u>Contingent remainder in fee</u> (unascertained owner and condition not met)
> >
> > O: Reversion

The first contingent remainder to B's youngest child is valid because we will know who B's youngest child is when B dies, making B the validating life.

For the second contingent remainder, the Rule in Shelley's case changes the owner of the interest without removing the condition precedent, so the final language of the grant would effectively read: "then if B's youngest child's heirs are adults, to B's youngest child." While we will know whether B's youngest child's heirs are adults at the time of B's youngest child's death (the expiration of his life estate), it is possible that B's youngest child is not a life in being at the time of the grant and that this person could die more than 21 years after all the lives in being (O, A, and B) have died. The second contingent remainder is therefore invalid under the RAP. This is true even if contingent remainders are destructible, because even though the remainder would have to vest by the expiration of the preceding estate, that estate is the life estate owned by B's youngest child, who may not be a life in being. *The state of title is*:

> A: Life estate
>
> B: Vested remainder in life estate
>
> B's youngest child: Contingent remainder in life estate (unascertained owner)
>
> O: Reversion

Provide the state of title (both before and after the RAP, and at each factual development along the way) for the conveyances in problems 19 and 20. Assume that the Rule in Shelley's Case and the Doctrine of Worthier Title apply. If it makes a difference whether contingent remainders are destructible, or whether there is a statute of limitations on Possibilities of Reverter and Rights of Entry, then provide alternative answers.

19. O to A for life, then to A's children who reach age 20 for life, then to B, but if O has a grandchild who reaches 20, then at that time to that grandchild (O has one child, C, who is 10, and A has no children).

> *Face of the grant*:
>
> > A: Life estate subject to an executory limitation
> >
> > A's children who reach age 20: <u>Contingent remainder in life estate subject to an executory limitation</u> (unascertained owner)
> >
> > B: Vested remainder, subject to divestment, in fee simple subject to an executory limitation
> >
> > O's grandchild who reaches age 20: <u>Shifting executory interest in fee</u>

The contingent remainder is valid under the RAP because we will know if A's children reach 20 less than 21 years after A dies. A is therefore a validating life. However, the RAP invalidates the executory interest because O's first grandchild who eventually turns 20 could be born more than one year after all lives in being have died (and thus the grandchild might not turn 20 until more than 21 years after all lives in being have died). O could have another child who is the grandchild's parent, and the grandchild could be born after O, A, and B have all died.

After the RAP:

A: Life estate

A's children who reach age 20: <u>Contingent remainder in life estate</u> (unascertained owner)

B: Vested remainder in fee

a.   Five years after the grant, A has a child, D.

Nothing changes; D doesn't own the remainder because he has not met the definition of ownership (a child of A who turns 20).

b.   Three years after D is born, A dies.

The answer here depends on whether contingent remainders are destructible. If they are, then the contingent remainder is destroyed for failure to vest by the expiration of the preceding estate. B's remainder would then become possessory and B would own the property in fee.

If contingent remainders are not destructible, then the contingent remainder can continue as an executory interest to see if any child of A turns 20 (which, again, would happen, if at all, within 21 years of A's death, under normal biological reproduction). The Rule of Convenience does not apply here because that rule only applies when at least one member of a class interest is entitled to take possession, and that is not true here. The next vested interest, B's remainder, would become possessory as a fee simple subject to an executory limitation (the turning of 20 by a child of A), which would be followed by a shifting executory interest for life own by the children of A who turn 20, followed by a vested remainder in fee owned by B.

d.   25 years after the grant, D turns 20.

Again, if contingent remainders are destructible, B owns a fee. If they are not, D now owns a life estate (with the class closed via the Rule of Convenience), and B owns a vested remainder in fee.

e.   Twenty years after D turns 20, C's first child, E, turns 20.

The RAP invalidated the interest of O's first grandchild to turn 20, so nothing changes. This answer does not depend on the existence of statutes of limitations, which typically apply only to possibilities of reverter and rights of entry, not to executory interests.

20. O to A for life as long as A lives in Virginia, then to B for life as long as B lives in Virginia.

Face of the grant:

A: Life estate determinable

B: <u>Shifting executory interest in life estate pur autre vie determinable</u>

B: Vested remainder in life estate determinable

O: Possibility of reverter (for the life of A—in the event B dies before A and then A moves away from Virginia)

O: Possibility of reverter (for the life of B—in the event that B takes possession and then moves away from Virginia)

O: Reversion

CH. 11   ANSWERS TO CHAPTER PRACTICE PROBLEMS

B's executory interest survives the RAP because the defeasance clause connected to A's interest will be violated only within A's lifetime, and thus A is a validating life.

a. A lives in Virginia for 35 years, then moves to New Hampshire. B does not live in Virginia when A moves to New Hampshire.

> This depends on whether the jurisdiction has a statute of limitations limiting the existence of possibilities of reverter from the time they are created. If so, and if the statutory period has run, even though B's executory interest is still valid, the statute of limitations eliminated O's possibility of reverter. Although A loses the property because A no longer lives in Virginia, B's executory interest still becomes possessory despite his violation of the defeasance clause. *Thus*:

> B: Life estate for the lives of A and B

> O: Reversion

> If, however, the jurisdiction does not have such a statute of limitations, or the statutory period has not yet run, then both A and B lose their interests because they violated their defeasance clauses. O regains the property through the possibility of reverter, which merges with the reversion. *Thus*:

> O: Fee

b. 5 years after A moves to New Hampshire, B moves to Virginia.

> This does not affect the title at all. If B already owns the property (as a life estate) because of the statute of limitations on possibilities of reverter, then his subsequent move to Virginia doesn't matter. On the other hand, if the possibility of reverter applied, B's interest was extinguished when he violated his own condition after A violated A's condition, and B cannot get his interest back now by complying with the provision.

Answer problem 21.

21. Oliver is a diehard fan of the newest NFL team, the England Tories, and has a house one block away from Schick Stadium, the venue where the Tories play "home" games in the U.S. Oliver has to move away for a job and wants his best friend, Alex, who is also a Tories fan, to have the house for his lifetime so he can easily attend Tories' games. But Oliver wants the house back if the Tories no longer play at Schick Stadium. Oliver's other friend Bill is a fan of quarterback Tom Trelow, so if Trelow helps the Tories win the Super Bowl, Oliver wants Bill to have the house. He thinks he can handle the transfer without an attorney, so he drafts the following conveyance: "I, Oliver, convey my House near Schick Stadium to Alex for his lifetime as long as the Tories play at Schick Stadium. Otherwise, the House will become mine again and I will have the right to reclaim it. If the Tories win the Super Bowl while Tom Trelow is on the team, then at that time my house will belong to Bill." Has Oliver accomplished his goals? What is the state of the title?

> Oliver's conveyance is unclear on several points. First, it appears to have created a life estate determinable for Alex, but then it provides what appears to be a right of entry. The law prefers the right of entry to the possibility of reverter, so this ambiguity would be resolved in favor of a life estate subject to a condition subsequent. The grant then provides an executory limitation and executory interest. It appears that Alex owns a life estate subject to both a

condition subsequent and an executory limitation, with Oliver owning a right of entry and a reversion and Bill owning a shifting executory interest in fee. The executory interest is valid under the RAP because it will be tested during Tom Trelow's lifetime, making him the validating life.

CHAPTER 9

In problems 1 and 2, provide the state of title under every approach to the fee tail.

1. O conveys Blueacre to A and the heirs of her body, but if A uses Blueacre for industrial purposes, then to B.

    Common law:

    > A: Fee tail subject to an executory limitation

    > B: Shifting executory interest in fee

    > O: Reversion

    Modern law (completely abolishing the fee tail):

    > A: Fee simple subject to an executory limitation

    > B: Shifting executory interest in fee

    Modern law (imposing a one-generation condition):

    The grant is construed to read: "to A as long as A does not die without a bodily heir, but if A uses Blueacre for industrial purposes, then to B."

    > A: Fee simple determinable

    > B: Shifting executory interest in fee

    > O: Possibility of reverter

2. O conveys Redacre to A and the heirs of his body, then to B and his heirs. A subsequently conveys to C and his heirs. Explain fully how you would assess who now owns what interests in Redacre.

    Common Law (on the face of the grant):

    > A: Fee tail

    > B: Vested remainder in fee

    Under the common law, A can only convey a life interest (for the life of A). *Therefore*:

    > C: Life estate pur autre vie (for the life of A)

    > A's heirs: Contingent remainder in fee tail

    > B: Vested remainder in fee

    Today, in the states that still recognize the traditional fee tail, the conveyance to C would have disentailed the fee tail, destroying B's interest. Accordingly, C would own fee simple.

    Modern Law (completely abolishing the fee tail):

    > A: Fee simple absolute

    After A conveys the interest to C, C owns Redacre in fee.

    Modern law (imposing a one-generation requirement):

The grant is construed to read: "to A as long as A does not die without a bodily heir, then to B and his heirs."

A: Fee simple determinable

B: Shifting executory interest in fee

After A conveys the interest to C, C owns Redacre in fee simple determinable and B still owns the shifting executory interest in fee.

Assume that your jurisdiction has adopted the USRAP and applies the Rule in Shelley's Case and the Doctrine of Worthier Title. Provide the state of title for the conveyances in problems 3–11. If it makes a difference whether contingent remainders are destructible, provide both answers.

3. O conveys Blackacre to A for life, then to B if the land is farmed for the next 90 years.

    Face of the grant:

    A: Life estate

    B: <u>Contingent remainder in fee</u>

    O: Reversion

    Applying the USRAP:

    Step 1: If contingent remainders are destructible, then B's remainder is valid and A is a validating life. If they are not destructible, then B's contingent remainder fails Step 1 because it cannot vest until 90 years of farming have passed, which might be more than 21 years after the death of the last life in being.

    Step 2: B's contingent remainder is guaranteed to fail or to vest within 90 years, and it is valid under the USRAP, and we wait and see what happens.

4. O conveys Blackacre to A for life, then to B, but if there is a manned mission to Mars within 80 years, then to the first astronaut to set foot on Mars.

    Face of the grant:

    A: Life estate

    B: Vested remainder, subject to divestment, in fee subject to an executory limitation

    First astronaut to set foot on Mars: <u>Shifting executory interest in fee</u>

    Applying the USRAP:

    Step 1: Even if the first astronaut to set foot on Mars does so within 80 years, this might be more than 21 years after the death of the last life in being. Therefore, the shifting executory interest fails Step 1.

    Step 2: The shifting executory interest only cuts off B's interest if the mission occurs within 80 years, so this satisfies Step 2, the interest is valid, and we wait and see what happens.

5. O conveys Blackacre to A for life, then to O's grandchildren who reach age 50 (O has no grandchildren).

    Face of the grant:

    A: Life estate

O's grandchildren who reach age 50: <u>Contingent remainder in fee</u>

O: Reversion

Applying the USRAP:

Step 1: If contingent remainders are destructible, then the contingent remainder is saved because A is the validating life. Otherwise, the contingent remainder fails Step 1.

Step 2: O might not have grandchildren who reach age 50 for more than 90 years. The contingent remainder fails Step 2.

Step 3: Wait and see whether the contingent remainder vests or ceases to exist within the next 90 years.

6. O conveys Blackacre to A in fee tail, then to O's issue alive at the time A's fee tail expires.

Face of the grant (common law):

A: Fee tail

O's issue alive at the time A's fee tail expires: <u>Contingent remainder in fee (the Doctrine of Worthier Title does not apply because this interest was not conveyed to O's heirs)</u>

O: Reversion

Applying the USRAP:

Step 1: Because A's fee tail could expire at some indefinite time in the future, the contingent remainder is not valid under the common law RAP.

Step 2: There is no express wait and see savings clause of 90 years or less, so the remainder fails Step 2.

Step 3: Wait and see whether the contingent remainder vests or ceases to exist within the next 90 years.

Modern law (abolishing the fee tail):

A: Fee

Modern law (imposing a one-generation requirement):

The grant is construed to read: "to A as long as A does not die without a bodily heir, then to O's issue then alive."

A: Fee simple determinable

O's issue then alive: <u>Shifting executory interest in fee</u>

Applying the USRAP:

Step 1: The executory interest meets Step 1 because it will be tested at A's death.

7. O conveys Blackacre to A, but if drought prevents the land from being farmed, then O may enter and reclaim Blackacre.

Face of the grant:

A: Fee subject to a condition subsequent

O: Right of entry

The USRAP does not apply to rights of entry.

8. O conveys Blackacre to A, but if A or A's issue ever runs for public office, then to B, if B is then living.

    Face of the grant:

    A: Fee subject to an executory limitation

    B: <u>Shifting executory interest in fee</u>

    Applying the USRAP:

    Step 1: Although A's issue might run for public office long after the deaths of each life in being, the savings clause ensures that B's interest will only become possessory within B's lifetime. Therefore, B is his own validating life, and B's executory interest is valid under Step 1.

9. O conveys Blackacre to A for life, then to B if B has grandchildren, otherwise to C (B has no grandchildren).

    Face of the grant:

    A: Life estate

    B: <u>Contingent remainder in fee</u>

    C: <u>Alternative contingent remainder in fee</u>

    O: Reversion

    Applying the USRAP:

    Step 1: If destructibility applies, A is the validating life and both contingent remainders are valid; otherwise, they both fail Step 1 because B's grandchildren might not be born for more than 21 years after the death of every life in being.

    Step 2: If destructibility does not apply, both contingent remainders fail Step 2 because there is no express wait and see savings clause for up to 90 years.

    Step 3: Wait and see whether B has grandchildren within the next 90 years.

10. O conveys Blackacre to A for life, then to B when B adopts A's children.

    Face of the grant:

    A: Life estate

    O: Reversion in fee subject to an executory limitation

    B: <u>Springing executory interest in fee</u>

    Applying the USRAP:

    Step 1: B's executory interest is valid because it will either become possessory or cease to exist within B's lifetime.

11. O conveys Blackacre to A as long as B lives, then to C.

    Face of the grant:

    This grant is ambiguous. If the presumption in favor of a fee controls, A owns a fee simple determinable, and C owns a shifting executory interest in fee, for which B is the validating life. The grant could be construed to convey a life estate pur autre vie (for the life of B) to A, with C owning a vested remainder in fee.

CHAPTER 10

Problems 1–16 include an initial conveyance, and some then provide a series of subsequent factual developments. Analyze the state of the title at the time of the grant and then at each point in the chronological chain of events. If necessary, apply the common law RAP. Explain at each point if your answer depends on different approaches to a relevant legal concept.

1. O to D for life as long as she remains single, then upon D's death to S and his heirs.

    a. At the time of the grant, D and S are alive; D is single.

    > D: Life estate determinable

    > O: Possibility of reverter (for the life of D)

    > S: Vested remainder in fee

    > S has a vested remainder because he will definitely get Blackacre in fee when D dies. O has a possibility of reverter, which will entitle him to get D's life estate back if D gets married. This illustrates how this possibility of reverter differs from one following a fee.

    b. D marries.

    > O: Life estate for the life of D

    > S: Vested remainder in fee

    > This fact sequence demonstrates how the defeasible language does not cut off the remainder. The remainder is not subject to divestment.

    c. D dies.

    > S: Fee

2. O to A for life, then to B for life if B marries C, then to A's heirs.

    Face of the grant:

    > A: Life estate

    > B: <u>Contingent remainder for life</u>

    > A's heirs: <u>Contingent remainder in fee</u>

    > O: Reversion

    A's heirs' interest is contingent because they are unascertained (until A dies). O has a reversion because the last interest is contingent.

    The two contingent remainders must be tested by the RAP—both are valid because they have explicit validating lives; B must marry C while both he and C are alive, and we will know A's heir(s) at A's death.

    The fact that O granted a life estate to A and in the same grant conveyed a remainder to A's heirs implicates the Rule in Shelley's Case. If that rule has been abolished, the above result stands. *If the rule applies*:

    > A: Life estate

    > B: Contingent remainder for life

    > A: Vested remainder in fee

    Even if contingent remainders are destructible, A's interests do not merge to destroy B's contingent remainder because the interests are created in one grant, not by a series of grants.

3. O to J as long as an Eastern State University graduate is not selected to serve as President of Western State University, then to A and her heirs (an ESU graduate has never been selected to serve as President of WSU).

> *If the court would presume O intended to convey a fee interest to J, then on the face of the grant*:
>
> > J: Fee simple determinable
> >
> > A: <u>Shifting executory interest in fee</u>
>
> However, the executory interest is void under the RAP, because it is based on a potentially perpetual condition not connected to any life in being. (If the USRAP applies, we must wait 90 years to see if an ESU graduate is selected to serve as President of WSU and thus if A's executory interest becomes possessory.) *Under the common law RAP, the final result is*:
>
> > J: Fee simple determinable
> >
> > O: Possibility of reverter (may be limited in time by modern statute)
>
> Note, however, that O used words of limitation to describe A's interest but not J's. It's possible a court might take this to mean O intended J's interest to be in a life estate, not a fee. *If so*:
>
> > J: Life estate determinable
> >
> > A: <u>Shifting executory interest for the life of J</u> (if the condition is violated)
> >
> > A: Vested remainder in fee (when J dies)
>
> Under this approach, A's executory interest is valid because it can only cut off J's life interest, and thus J is the validating life.

4. O to A when communism collapses in North Korea.

> *Face of the grant*:
>
> > O: Fee simple subject to an executory limitation
> >
> > A: <u>Springing executory interest in fee</u>
>
> This potentially perpetual condition is not connected to any life in being (if the USRAP applies, we would wait up to 90 years to see if the condition is met). *The resulting state of the title under the RAP is*:
>
> > O: Fee (a meaningless conveyance)

5. O to A for life, then to B and his heirs, but if B fails to live to 50, then to C and his heirs (B is 10).

> *Face of the grant*:
>
> > A: Life estate
> >
> > B: Vested remainder, subject to divestment, in fee subject to an executory limitation
> >
> > C: <u>Shifting executory interest in fee</u>
>
> C's executory interest is valid under the RAP because C's interest will become possessory, if at all, either at A's death or at B's death, making A and B the validating lives.

6. O to A for the life of Q, then to B and his heirs if B marries C.

   a. At the time of the grant, B is unmarried.

       A: Life estate pur autre vie

       B: <u>Contingent remainder in fee</u>

       O: Reversion

       B's contingent remainder is valid under the RAP—B and C are validating lives because they can only get married while both are alive.

   b. O sells his remaining interest in Blackacre to A.

     If contingent remainders are destructible:

       A: Fee (via merger)

     If not:

       A: Life estate pur autre vie

       B: Contingent remainder in fee

       A: Reversion

7. O to A for life, then to B and his heirs, but if the land is ever used for commercial purposes, then to Royal University and its successors and assigns.

     Face of the grant:

       A: Life estate

       B: Vested remainder, subject to divestment, in fee subject to an executory limitation

       RU: <u>Shifting executory interest in fee</u>

     Even though the commercial purpose condition could be violated during A's ownership, A's life estate is not defeasible because the grant does not expressly say that a violation of the condition will cut off A's life estate (e.g., it doesn't say "then at that time").

     RU's executory interest is void under the RAP because the condition is potentially perpetual (must wait and see for 90 years if the USRAP applies). We must strike both the executory interest and the condition that precedes it. *Thus, the state of the title under the RAP is*:

       A: Life estate

       B: Vested remainder in fee

     This reflects how the RAP can affect vested remainders subject to divestment. *Compare the next problem*:

8. O to A for life, then to B and his heirs so long as the land is not used for commercial purposes, then to Royal University and its successors and assigns.

     Face of the grant:

       A: Life estate

       B: Vested remainder in fee simple determinable

       RU: <u>Shifting executory interest in fee</u>

Again, RU's executory interest is void under the RAP. However, here we can strike the executory interest without changing B's interest. *The resulting state of the title is*:

    A: Life estate

    B: Vested remainder in fee simple determinable

    O: Possibility of reverter (may be limited in time by statute)

9. O to A for life, then if a person walks on Mars, to B and his heirs.

    Face of the grant:

        A: Life estate

        B: <u>Contingent remainder in fee</u>

        O: Reversion

    Whether B's contingent remainder is valid depends on whether contingent remainders are destructible.

    If they are, the remainder is valid because it must vest by A's death or be destroyed, so A is the validating life.

    If contingent remainders are not destructible, the remainder is void because B's interest could continue on indefinitely as an executory interest after A dies. *If so, the resulting state of the title is*:

        A: Life estate

        O: Reversion

10. O to A for life, then to B's first-born child for life, then if Texas has seceded from the union, to C and his heirs. Analyze this grant under two alternative factual scenarios:

    a. At the time of the grant, B has children.

        Face of the grant:

            A: Life estate

            B's first-born: Vested remainder for life

            C: <u>Contingent remainder in fee</u>

            O: Reversion

        C's contingent remainder is valid under the RAP because B's first-born is a life in being, and the condition must be tested at that child's death ("if Texas *has* seceded. . ."). B's first-born is thus the validating life.

    b. At the time of the grant, B does not have children.

        Face of the grant:

            A: Life estate

            B's first-born: <u>Contingent remainder for life</u>

            C: <u>Contingent remainder in fee</u>

            O: Reversion

        B's first-born's remainder is valid under the RAP because it must vest, if at all, during B's life (B's first-born child would be born while B is alive, or within 9 months of B's death if B is a man, so B is the validating life).

However, C's contingent remainder is now void. Given that B has no children, B's first-born is not a life in being, and there is no other validating life for C's interest. *The resulting state of the title after RAP is:*

> A: Life estate
>
> B's first-born: Contingent remainder for life
>
> O: Reversion

11. O to A for life, then to B as long as B farms Blackacre.

> A: Life estate
>
> B: Vested remainder in fee simple determinable
>
> O: Possibility of reverter

12. O to A for life, then to B if B maintained the property for A.

> *Face of the grant:*
>
> > A: Life estate
> >
> > B: <u>Contingent remainder in fee</u>
> >
> > O: Reversion

The contingent remainder is valid under the RAP because we will know whether B maintained the property for A either at A's death or B's death. If A dies first, we will test the condition at his death. If B dies first, the grant does not require B to maintain the property for all of A's life, so presumably that would not be a problem provided B so maintained the property before his death. If contingent remainders are destructible, that provides a second reason why A is a validating life.

13. O to A in fee tail, then to B for life if B marries C, then to D.

> *Face of the grant:*
>
> > A: Fee tail
> >
> > B: <u>Contingent remainder in life estate</u>
> >
> > D: Vested remainder in fee (NOT alternative contingent)

B and C are expressly the validating lives for B's contingent remainder.

14. O to A for life, then to B for life, then to C, but if C lives alone on the property, then to O.

> A: Life estate
>
> B: Vested remainder in life estate
>
> C: Vested remainder in fee subject to a condition subsequent
>
> O: Right of entry

15. O to A for life, but if A stops attending church every Sunday, then to B for life, then if C ever attends church, to C.

> *Face of the grant:*
>
> > A: Life estate subject to an executory limitation
> >
> > B: <u>Shifting executory interest in life estate</u>

C: <u>Contingent remainder in fee</u> (note that C's remainder follows A's life estate if it naturally expires, or, if B's executory interest cuts A's interest off, then C's interest follows B's life estate)

O: Reversion

Both A and B are validating lives for B's executory interest—because it's for life, it cannot exist beyond B's death, and also the condition involves A's actions and thus must be tested during A's lifetime (and thus finally at A's death). C is the validating life for C's remainder because the condition involves C's own actions; furthermore, if remainders are destructible, the condition must be met by the death of A and B or the remainder will be destroyed, making A and B validating lives for B's contingent remainder.

16. O to A as long as any of O's children are alive and younger than 21, then to B (O has one child, C, who is 9).

Face of the grant:

A: Fee simple determinable

B: <u>Shifting executory interest in fee</u>

Whether the RAP invalidates the interest depends on whether O is a woman or a man.

If O is a woman, her last child would have to turn 21 no later than 21 years after her death (the worst case scenario, given normal biological reproduction, is that she would die giving birth). That would make O the validating life, and the state of the title would stand.

If O is a man, B's interest is invalid. Although the RAP allows an extra 9 months to determine whether an individual is a life in being, that rule does not help here. The condition expressly requires that the child of O be alive and younger than 21, which could happen more than 21 years after O dies. That means O cannot be the validating life if O is a man. The condition is not tied to any of the other lives in being (A, B, or C), so they would not be validating lives either. *That would leave the state of the title*:

A: Fee simple determinable

O: Possibility of reverter

For problems 17–18, first give the state of title on the face of the grant. Identify any interests that are threatened by the RAP. Test the interests, and give the state of title after applying the RAP. Apply the Rule in Shelley's Case as applicable. Assume contingent remainders are not destructible.

17. O to A for life, then to O's last daughter to graduate college (O is 90 years old; she has five children, all of whom have graduated college; Z was the most recent daughter to so graduate).

Face of the grant:

A: Life estate

O's last daughter to graduate from college: <u>Contingent remainder in fee simple absolute (unascertained owner)</u>

O: Reversion

If contingent remainders are destructible, A is the validating life because the remainder will be destroyed at A's death if it has not yet vested. If they are not destructible, the remainder is void. The law looks at what is possible, not at what is probable. After making the conveyance, O could have another daughter. This daughter might graduate college more than 21 years after the death of the last life in being. *Therefore, the contingent remainder is void and the state of title is*:

> A: Life estate
>
> O: Reversion

18. O to A for life, then to B if B's grandchildren graduate high school (none of B's grandchildren have yet graduated high school).

> *Face of the grant*:
>
> > A: Life estate
> >
> > B: Contingent remainder in fee simple absolute (unsatisfied condition precedent)
> >
> > O: Reversion
>
> If contingent remainders are not destructible, B's interest is void, because the remainder could continue as an executory interest after A dies (and his life estate expires), and the grandchildren might not graduate high school until more than 21 years after the death of every life in being (O, A, and B). *Therefore, the state of title is*:
>
> > A: Life estate
> >
> > O: Reversion

Determine the state of title after each event in problem 19. If you do not have enough information to determine the state of title after every event, explain why.

19. O conveys Blackacre to A for life, then to B as long as the property is used during B's lifetime for residential purposes. After A dies, B begins residing on the sprawling estate. Nonetheless, sensing economic opportunity when the population in a nearby city expands, B develops Blackacre and turns it into a shopping center.

> *Time of the grant*:
>
> > A: Life estate
> >
> > B: Vested remainder in fee simple determinable
> >
> > O: Possibility of reverter
>
> *After A's death*:
>
> > B: Fee simple determinable
> >
> > O: Possibility of reverter
>
> *After B develops Blackacre*:
>
> > To determine whether O's possibility of reverter took effect, you must know whether the jurisdiction has a statute of limitations for possibilities of reverter, how long the statute of limitations is for, and whether the period of time has passed. If the statute of limitations has run, then B possesses fee simple absolute; otherwise, O now owns a fee.

Problems 20–24 build on concepts you have already learned, testing how deeply you can analyze their implications. These problems are difficult, and do not be surprised if you cannot determine all the answers. Determine the state of title.

20. O to A for life, then to B for life if B is then an adult, then to A's heirs as long as O does not die before O's children reach adulthood, then to O's heirs.

    Face of the grant:

    A: Life estate

    B: <u>Contingent remainder in life estate</u>

    A's heirs: <u>Contingent remainder in fee simple determinable</u>

    O's heirs: <u>Shifting executory interest in fee</u>

    After the Rule in Shelley's Case and the Doctrine of Worthier Title:

    A: Life estate

    B: <u>Contingent remainder in life estate</u>

    A: Vested remainder in fee simple determinable

    O: Possibility of reverter

    B's contingent remainder is valid under the RAP because the condition will be tested at A's death, making A the validating life (and if contingent remainders are destructible, that is another reason why A is the validating life). Notably, A's interests do *not* merge and destroy B's contingent remainder because they were created in the same grant.

    What if A dies while B is an adult, and then O dies before O's children reach adulthood? B would own a life estate, and A's devisee or heir would own a vested remainder in fee simple determinable. However, notice that the defeasance clause is already definitively violated. When B dies, the next vested interest, A's remainder, would become possessory, but then it would be immediately cut off due to the violation of the condition. This is like a contingent remainder never vesting and thus never becoming possessory, but here A's remainder is subject to a determinable clause, not a condition precedent, and so it is vested, not contingent. For this reason, O retained only a possibility of reverter, and not also a reversion. Nevertheless, given this sequence of events, in the end, title would revert to O.

21. O conveys Greenacre to A and his heirs in fee simple for his lifetime.

    This language is ambiguous on its face because it could create either a life estate or a fee. However, the law prefers a fee over an expirable estate, so this ambiguity should be resolved in favor of a fee simple.

22. T devises Blackacre to A for life, then to T's children if they reach age 20 (T has three children, B, C, and D, but only B has reached age 20 by the time T dies). Before C or D reach 20, they—along with A—drown in the storm surge of a category 5 hurricane. Only B survives. (Hint: do you see the ambiguity?).

    T's children have a remainder, and it is contingent because of a condition precedent—they must reach age 20. Arguably, a literal reading of the grant requires *all* of them to reach age 20 ("if <u>they</u> reach 20") before the remainder vests. A looser reading would interpret this as a class gift (i.e., "then to T's children *who* reach age 20"). Under the latter approach, the remainder is vested subject to open. The law prefers vested remainders over contingent ones, but in this case a literal reading suggests the remainder is contingent; accordingly, the correct outcome is unclear.

State of title:

>   A: Life estate
>
>   T's children: Contingent remainder in fee
>
>   T's devisee/heir: Reversion

OR

>   A: Life estate
>
>   B: Vested remainder subject to open in fee

After A, C, and D drown, then either T's heirs/devisees own the fee or B owns fee.

23. T writes a will leaving Blackacre to A for life, then to A's heirs. A dies. Then T dies.

> At first glance, the Rule in Shelley's Case might seem applicable. Remember, however, that the will is not effective until T dies. At that point, the devise to A for life is ineffective because A is already dead. In effect, the devise does *not* pass an interest to A and to A's heirs—it only passes an estate to A's heirs. Accordingly, the Rule in Shelley's Case is inapplicable.

> Because the devise to A's heirs is proper but the devise to A is ineffective, A's heirs own a present estate at T's death. Given that A is dead, A's heirs would be ascertainable (although we have not been given enough information to identify the actual heirs). Thus, A's heir(s) own(s) a fee.

24. O grants Blackacre to A while A is living, but if A dies O may enter and reclaim.

> This conveyance is ambiguous. The interest to A is presumptively in fee, but the defeasance clause makes it essentially a life interest. The interest following should be a reversion if it follows a life estate, but it is written as a right of entry. It is not certain how a court would interpret this; however, the presumptions in favor of a fee simple and against automatic forfeiture would most likely lead a court to hold that this is a fee subject to a condition subsequent, followed by a right of entry. If so, when A dies, O would have the right to enter and reclaim, and if O does not do so (within the statute of limitations), the property should pass to A's devisee/heir in fee.

INDEX

References are to Pages
